An Unusual Brief

The Life and Times of a High Street Lawyer

– ROGER TERRELL –

An environmentally friendly book printed and bound in England by
www.printondemand-worldwide.com

Mixed Sources
Product group from well-managed
forests, and other controlled sources
www.fsc.org Cert no. TT-COC-002641
© 1996 Forest Stewardship Council
FSC

PEFC Certified
This product is
from sustainably
managed forests
and controlled
sources
www.pefc.org
PEFC
PEFC/16-33-415

This book is made entirely of chain-of-custody materials

Roger Terrell

www.fast-print.net/store.php

An Unusual Brief - The Life and Times of a High Street Lawyer
Copyright © Roger Terrell 2012

This book is a work of non-fiction, based on the life experiences and recollections of the author, Roger
Terrell. In some cases, the names of people have been changed to protect their privacy. The author has
stated to the publishers that, except in such respects, the contents of this book are true and accurate
according to his memory and recollection of events.

The author and publishers have made every reasonable effort to contact copyright holders for
permission to use photographs and believe that the credits given are accurate.

ISBN 978-178035-226-8

First published 2012 by
FASTPRINT PUBLISHING
Peterborough, England.

Roger Terrell

"AN UNUSUAL BRIEF"

Roger Terrell was born, brought up and educated in Peterborough. After completing his law degree and law society exams, he embarked upon a training contract in the legal department at Nottinghamshire County Council in West Bridgford, Nottingham. Upon qualification, he married and returned to the Peterborough area, working in private practice and gaining basic knowledge in the essential skills of a high street lawyer.

He enjoyed a sideways move to the legal department of a multinational, public quoted, engineering group named Baker Perkins. In May 1988, he decided to set up his own high street practice dealing with criminal and family law, commercial contractual matters, conveyancing, wills and probate. Over the next twenty-five years, he became involved in a number of cases, which made national and local headlines. Through his clients, he became involved in professional football and later became a director and then chairman of Peterborough United Football Club, (The Posh). He also operated as a professional football players, FIFA registered, agent.

He has a weekly question and answer column in the Peterborough Evening Telegraph called 'Is it Legal?' He has written articles for a number of legal journals and has appeared on national and local television, radio and in newspapers in connection with his professional, legal work and football related matters, many of these experiences being recounted in this book.

LIST OF CHAPTERS

1. Getting Qualified

My father Frank (nicknamed Pat), and mother Maisie, owned and ran a farm at Yaxley in Huntingdonshire from a huge rambling Victorian farmhouse called The Grange, which was set in about six acres of gardens, farm buildings and paddocks and, of course, had the compulsory Aga in the kitchen. I was brought up at The Grange with my older brother Frank and younger sister Claire. We had an idyllic childhood, except that my father was always trying to get us to do chores around the farm, like collecting eggs or working in the potato and sugar beet fields. He would always pay us so there was never any question of pocket money. A work ethic was instilled in us to get up early and work hard and success would come our way. We lived in one of those old fashioned communities in the sixties where nobody locked their front doors, everybody knew their neighbours and all children, including ourselves and our friends would spend the school holidays at the local recreation ground "the Rec" playing, depending on the season, football or cricket. For some reason everybody had a nickname; Whack, Blossom, Bucket. Mine was of course Roger the Dodger or Dodge. I attended normal state schools and the good thing about Huntingdonshire was that it was the second smallest county in England after Rutland, with only the small market towns of Huntingdon, Ramsey, St Ives and St Neots, so it was much easier to get in the county team for football and cricket, which I did! I am sure that Yorkshire, Lancashire and Middlesex would have been more testing.

As I approached the age of eighteen in the final year of my 'A' level studies at Orton Longueville School near Peterborough I had to make a decision – what job/career do I want to pursue? Although having some football and cricket potential, I soon realised that I was not going to make it as a professional sportsman and then my father suggested law. I thought it was a good idea but I would have thought any suggestion was a good idea as I had no clue as to what I wanted to do in life. I got the grades and went off on a three year degree course in Nottingham. As part of the course I undertook two periods of work experience at local firms in Peterborough. The first session was at a traditional medium-sized high street firm with very good standards called Jeffreys, Orrell & Co. Some of the partners were very stuffy and looked down on the staff. I remember Giles Jeffreys, the very autocratic senior partner, reprimanding me one afternoon as he had seen me eating chips at lunchtime. He thought clients would think badly of the firm (not me) if they saw me eating such food. In 1975 on the wages of £10.00 per week that they were paying, chips were about all I could afford at lunchtime!

For the second spell of work experience, I joined the then best firm in Peterborough, called Greenwoods. They were well organised and dynamic and gave me plenty of opportunity to earn fees with clients, even though I was inexperienced. I was under the supervision of a trainee/newly qualified solicitor called Robert Wardle, who later in his career went on to become the Head of the Serious Fraud Office, so very early on I had some good mentors. I soon learned the procedures around family law work: mainly divorce, custody issues and domestic violence, for mainly women clients funded by legal aid. Domestic violence in relationships was then and is still a huge problem and very difficult to tackle. I remember a lady coming to see me and her explaining to me that she lived in fear of her ex-partner as he was always pushing her around and making threats to kill her. They had separated temporarily and I explained to the lady that before we could issue Court proceedings for a non-molestation injunction against her ex-partner, we would have to write him a warning letter. She agreed and we sent out the warning letter. Two days later, at about 9.15am, the senior partner, Ray Laxton, called and asked me to come to his office. I was worried and could not think of anything obvious that I had done wrong. He

5

invited me into his office and asked me to sit down. "Did I act for….." and he gave me the name of the lady who had consulted me over her ex-partner's threats and domestic violence. I said I did and Mr Laxton said, "Well, unfortunately she was murdered by her ex-partner last night." When the ex-partner received my warning letter, he was so incensed he went round to her house and carried out his threat. Mr Laxton told me C.I.D officers from Cambridgeshire Constabulary would be seeing me later and taking a statement. I duly gave my statement but I was not called to give evidence as the ex-partner pleaded guilty to murder and was sentenced to life imprisonment. This was a very early example to me of the serious implications of threats made by ex-partners and how they should be dealt with by solicitors and the police.

On a lighter note, Greenwoods was a large office full of lovely young people with a sense of humour. I remember the reception staff playing a practical joke on one of the junior partners by filling in an application for Dateline on his behalf and letting him deal with the embarrassment this created before them coming clean that they had filled in the forms. I also remember being in my office one morning when reception put through a call from a Mrs Gotobed. Knowing of their previous antics, I said to Mrs Gotobed, "I know you are not a client, you are Sharon from reception just messing around." Mrs Gotobed insisted she was genuine and then I suddenly recalled that I had seen a Mrs Gotobed about three months earlier and she had told me that in the Crowland area in the Fens, Gotobed was quite a common surname! I apologised profusely; how embarrassing!

The advantage of a law degree is that if you like the subject it does take you along a well-defined path which is easy to follow, particularly if you want to become a solicitor. I liked the academic work and the practical experience and I went on to do the Law Society Part II examinations after my degree and was on the lookout for a training contract. The problem with training contracts was, and still is, that they are hard to come by and do not pay particularly well. I then saw an advertisement for a trainee solicitor with Nottinghamshire County Council based at County Hall in West Bridgeford, with an unbelievable salary for 1977 of £5,000 per annum, when the going rate in private practice was £2,000 per annum.

I applied for the job and got an interview. The senior solicitor in charge of recruitment was an awesome, young, dynamic and ambitious solicitor called John Hayes. He later became Secretary General of the Law Society. He was also a cricket fanatic and when I told him about my one very brief appearance for Huntingdonshire Under-16s, he seemed totally impressed and forgot about academic legal stuff. He did not ask, and I did not tell him, that I only played one game and scored one and two not out. I was offered the job and accepted. My fiancée Cherry and I got married and purchased our first house in the Carlton district of Nottingham. The legal department at Nottinghamshire County Council was very lively, with a group of young trainees and newly qualified solicitors who wanted to get on and a group of less ambitious legal executives and clerks who had previously worked in private practice, never passed their exams and were just happy to be in a legal backwater with better than average pay, holidays, flexi-time etc. The majority of the staff did not take life too seriously and liked playing practical jokes. All the staff lived in fear of John Hayes, the solicitor who had originally interviewed me. I was doing my training stint in the conveyancing department when Ian James, one of the legal executives in that department put down his telephone and said, "That was John Hayes' secretary. He wants you in his office immediately. When John Hayes says 'jump', you ask 'how high?'". I shot off to his office, which was on the other side of the huge County Hall building. The door was closed and I knocked and went in. "What do you want?" asked John Hayes. "You wanted to see me sir?" "Did I? No, I do not want to see you," replied John Hayes. At that moment, I realised I had been set up. I walked slowly back through the County Hall corridors to my desk in the conveyancing department. When I entered the room, there were cheers and hoots of derision; everybody thought the set up had been hilarious. From that day, I was very cautious about anything I was told by Ian James and any members of the conveyancing department.

As I approached the end of my training contract, I needed to be thinking about what I would be doing once I qualified. My wife,

Cherry, was working at The Boots Company in Beeston and had a good, well-paid job and we were now well rooted in Nottingham. A job came up with Nottinghamshire Prosecuting Solicitors' Department on a very good salary. I went for an interview and was offered and accepted the job. I had kept in touch with a lot of my old football friends in the Peterborough area and we would regularly go back home and friends would regularly come and stay with us. One mate, Mike Moran, was an estate agent in Huntingdon and he knew a solicitor in St Ives, called Jeffrey Mills who was desperate to expand his business on the litigation side and open other offices in the area. I already had a job and I was quite happy with the way my life and career in Nottingham was going but I did meet Jeffrey Mills at his office in St Ives. I took him at face value. He seemed a nice man and talked a good game. He offered me £500 per annum more than Nottinghamshire Prosecuting Solicitors. This offer created a real dilemma for me and I discussed it in detail with Cherry. We could move back to the Peterborough area and both be close to our families. We could buy a much larger house and all in all it sounded a great opportunity. I spoke to Nottinghamshire Prosecuting Solicitors and told them that I had changed my mind. They were fine as they always had more applicants than vacancies. We put our house on the market in Carlton and it soon sold and we purchased a brand new house in Folksworth, just south of Peterborough. Cherry easily got a job at a research centre near Huntingdon. Everything slotted perfectly into place. Jeffrey Mills' practice in St Ives was very small and, as I soon found out, very disorganised. It was mainly conveyancing based and Mr Mills did not make it clear to me when I joined, but he expected me to find, from my own contacts, new work to develop the litigation side of his business and the opening of an office in Huntingdon. I did my best but I had been away from the area for three years and it takes a while to develop contacts and business referrals.

A very good footballing friend of mine called Colin Waters contacted me. He had been jointly charged, with another mate called Nigel Veni, with an offence of criminal damage to a car outside a dance at Yaxley Village Hall. I took Colin's instructions. He admitted he was there outside the dance but he did not kick the car as alleged and did not know who did. We were set for a trial at

Peterborough Magistrates' Court. I did tell Colin that I had just qualified and had never previously represented a client in a trial in the Magistrates' Court where there was to be live evidence and cross-examination of an experienced police officer who attended the scene and carried out the interviews.

The day of the trial arrived. I assured Colin we were all set and the prosecution opened their case and called their main witness, PC Leslie Woodbridge. Unbelievably, he was my first cousin and we had spent a lot of time together in our childhoods but I had lost touch with him over the previous four to five years. I did know through the family that he had joined the police force and was doing well. Nigel Veni, the co-accused, was represented by a barrister and their defence was exactly the same as ours. They did not kick the car and had no knowledge as to who did. When it came to cross-examination of Les, the barrister for Nigel Veni went first, asked only two or three questions and sat down. I stood up and asked exactly the same questions, using exactly the same words as the barrister and sat down. Both of us then made an application for the case to be dismissed through lack of evidence. Again, the barrister went first and my submission was couched in almost the same words as his. The Magistrates retired to consider their decision. About ten minutes later they came back and announced case dismissed against both defendants. We were all jubilant. My first contested trial, and a "not guilty"; what a great result. I did feel a little sorry for my cousin Les, but not for long. He subsequently went on to have a long and distinguished career with Cambridgeshire Constabulary and the Regional Crime Squad.

In May, after three months with Jeffrey Mills, I had gained a fair amount of new business and was seeing my work load develop quite nicely. We got to the last day of May and I decided to check with my bank and see if my salary cheque had been paid in. It had not. I thought this was very strange and before I approached Jeffrey Mills, I thought I would check with colleagues to see if they had been paid. They all had and I was furious. I stormed in to see Jeffrey Mills and asked him what the problem was as he had not paid me and not told me why. I had my mortgage and other payments due out of my account in the next couple of days. He was defensive and said he had cash flow problems and his son had an operation which he had to pay for that month. The reality was he just did not have the money or a proper business plan. I left my resignation on his desk and stormed out. Fine, but now I had no job and no income. The reality was that there were plenty of jobs around for newly qualified solicitors and I immediately got a job with a Stamford firm of solicitors, called Daltons, in their Lincoln Road, Peterborough office. They were good steady reliable people who would never let staff or clients down and for the next twelve to eighteen months I started building up my knowledge and experience as a litigation solicitor, dealing with all types of Court work: criminal, family and civil litigation. I liked the people, liked the work and generally the clients were not too bad either!

Whilst I had been undergoing my training contract at Nottinghamshire County Council, I was temporarily converted from being a Peterborough United football fan to following the fortunes of Nottingham Forest in their phenomenally successful period under Brian Clough when they won the League, Championship and two European Cups. My support of Nottingham Forest was particularly helped by me following a successful team and also by a trainee solicitor colleague of mine called Rob Severn who was a fanatical Forest fan, season ticket holder and organiser of my tickets and transport to all important Forest games. Even after we both left Nottinghamshire County Council, we both kept in touch and attended games together with a group of friends. Although their fortunes waned after I had moved away from Nottingham, they did reach the semi-final of the F.A Cup in April 1989 and were due to play the then mighty Liverpool at the neutral venue of Hillsborough, Sheffield, the home of Sheffield Wednesday Football Club. Rob organised the tickets and I met him and our usual group of friends and supporters at The Test Match pub in West Bridgford, Nottingham and then we all drove up and met appropriately at The Robin Hood pub in Sheffield and then onto the game. Football supporters are always optimistic about their team's prospects and we were all looking forward to an exciting game. The geography and road systems of Sheffield dictated that although Liverpool would have a larger following of supporters, they would have the Leppings Lane end and Nottingham Forest would have the Sheffield

Wednesday home end called ironically 'The Kop end.' We got to the stadium in plenty of time for the kick off and the match was a sell out. It was still the days of standing behind the goal. The teams came out; there was a great atmosphere and anticipation of an exciting game in front of a noisy, packed stadium with the customary singing and chanting. Where we were standing was full but it certainly was not packed or uncomfortable. The teams came out and the game kicked off with Liverpool attacking the Kop end where we were standing.

I remember very early on after only about five minutes, Liverpool got a corner and from the resulting cross Peter Beardsley had a shot which rattled the Forest cross bar. As is usual at a football match with this bit of excitement, the Liverpool crowd behind the goal at the Leppings Lane end surged forward. There was nothing unusual in that but then we could see the supporters at the Liverpool end in quite large numbers starting to climb over the safety fences. At first at the Forest end we thought this was just hooligan behaviour and was going to spoil the game. The players left the field of play. Then the supporters at the Liverpool end started breaking up advertising hoardings and carrying people away using these hoardings as stretchers. Nobody really knew what was happening but a few people had radios on and there were people saying that there had been a crush at the Liverpool end and people had been injured. Shortly after this, ambulances started arriving and actually coming into the stadium via an emergency entrance. Clearly there had been a very serious incident and we were notified over a public-address system that the game had been abandoned. As we started leaving the stadium we were disappointed the game had been called off but then the supporters with their portable radios were saying one or two people had died. We were stunned. Who could go to a football match on a Saturday afternoon and be killed? It was not possible. As we walked back to the car the death toll rose- three, nine, eleven. We could not believe what we were hearing. All these events were taking place before mobile telephones. Nobody had a mobile phone and if you were away from home you had to make a call from a telephone box and hope that the person you were calling was in and could take the call. I knew my wife had enough knowledge of football to know I was in the Forest end and all the problems were at the Liverpool end and so I was not unduly worried about calling her. If I had been worried, it would have been impossible in any event, as outside every phone box we passed in the Sheffield area there were queues of twenty or thirty people. As we listened to events unfolding whilst we drove back to Nottingham in the car, we just could not believe what we were hearing. We now know that the Hillsborough disaster on 15 April 1989 resulted in the deaths of ninety-six people and seven hundred and sixty-six being injured. It remains the deadliest stadium related disaster in British history and led to the introduction of all-seater stadiums in England.

2. *Engineering Experience in Industry and then how to Curry Favour in Pakistan*

In May 1982, I was sitting in the office, just looking through the solicitors' trade magazine, The Law Society's Gazette. As we all do, I looked at the job advertisements, not because I was looking for a job but just to see what was around. A job did catch my eye; not with a firm of solicitors, but a legal job for an engineering company based in Peterborough called Baker Perkins. Everybody in Peterborough knows of Baker Perkins. They were a well established, well respected firm employing over a thousand people at their site in Westfield Road, Peterborough. They were involved in the supply and manufacture of biscuit making and bakery equipment, foundry equipment and big web off-set printing presses used for printing high quality glossy magazines and books. The job involved dealing with all legal aspects of such a large diverse organisation, such as contractual negotiations and disputes, agency agreements, patents, trademarks and intellectual property; all really interesting subjects, which generally I knew nothing about and had no experience of. I telephoned the number shown in the advertisement, received and completed an application form and was called for an interview with Peter Dodd, the head of the legal department and company secretary.

I attended the huge office block for the interview and was ushered up to the third floor. This was a real contrast to the small private practice firm I was with, in size and content of work; a different world. Peter Dodd was a rotund, middle-aged public school educated barrister, who had been brought up in East Africa as his father was involved in the ill-fated Groundnuts Scheme in the 1950s. Peter was a lovely man but totally mad and eccentric and enjoyed hobbies like yachting and flying light aircraft. He needed an assistant, just someone with basic legal knowledge, and for some reason I fitted his bill exactly and I was offered the job on the spot. The pay was a little bit more but I had the opportunity of an interesting and totally different challenge to anything I ever anticipated would come my way. I started the job as solicitor and assistant company secretary and immediately started the induction programme which was very helpful in understanding how the business worked. I went to a biscuit making factory, United Biscuits at Harlesden in North London, and saw how McVities Jaffa Cakes and Digestive biscuits were made on Baker Perkins' equipment, and then on to a foundry and saw the most frightening and dangerous processes involved; molten metal flying around everywhere, accompanied by the heat and smell of sulphur and the noise of constant hammering. Back in the office, I was given the task of dealing with E.C.G.D claims. At the time, the value of properly approved exports of capital equipment to approved purchasers in approved countries would be insured by a government department called the Export Credits Guarantee Department (E.C.G.D). This department was set up to facilitate and promote British exports overseas and was extremely popular and successful. If the British exporter i.e. Baker Perkins properly complied with E.C.G.D and the purchasers defaulted, E.C.G.D would pay out ninety percent of the value of the payment defaulted upon. It was a condition of the arrangement that they would then require the British exporter, i.e. Baker Perkins, to pursue the defaulting party, usually through the Courts in their own country.

At the time, Baker Perkins had a very successful market for the sale of huge plant bakeries to Nigeria. The director in charge of the Bakery Division called me to his office one morning and explained the default by a company called Sunshine Bakeries in Lagos, Nigeria and the ongoing proceedings we had instituted in the Supreme Court of Lagos to enforce our debt. He told me I had better go out to Lagos and liaise with our solicitor there and make sure we were properly complying with E.C.G.D requirements. I was told, "Get out there as soon possible and report back." The first thing I had to do was attend at Addenbrookes Hospital for yellow fever vaccinations. I was in the waiting room and the nurse called me forward and asked me if I was a member of the Cambridge University Antarctic Expedition. I had to tell her unfortunately not, I was just going to Lagos on business! I spoke with a number of the sales team about Lagos and they all had really worrying stories about the food, hotels and general lawlessness of the place.

The next Sunday I was off to Gatwick on a British Airways flight to Lagos. I arrived at Murtala Muhammed Airport in the early evening, just as it was getting dark, and eventually got through the chaotic passport and customs control and there waiting for me was Billy, the Baker Perkins approved safe taxi driver who had looked after Baker Perkins' representatives in Lagos for years. I got in his taxi and we headed from the airport through the suburbs of Lagos towards the Mainland Hotel in the city centre. It was dark and there were no street lights. Suddenly, I could see blue flashing lights up ahead, people milling around and cars blocking the road. Billy brought the taxi to a halt and a man in a blue police uniform with Lagos Police badges and carrying a semi-automatic weapon opened the back of the taxi, pointed his gun at me, and ordered me out of the car. I did not know what was happening but immediately got out. There were about five agitated police officers standing around. They all carried semi-automatic weapons. "What have you got in there?" the police officer asked, pointing to my briefcase with his semi-automatic. "Papers. Have a look if you like." He ignored me and asked the same question in relation to my suitcase. I replied, "Clothes. Have a look if you like." He did not look but asked me where I was going and why I was there. I explained I was there on business and staying at the Mainland Hotel. He then pulled me to one side and said, "You give me ten naira" (about £10). I explained to him that I had just arrived in the country and did not have any local currency. This was true. He was very angry and said, pointing his gun at me, "You get in the car and go."

I was a bit shaken up by the incident and as we got going along the road, I asked Billy what that was all about. He just shrugged his shoulders and said it was a common occurrence. Young men would join the police, get the uniform, attend the Police Academy for a few days and then disappear. They would then get together with their friends, who had done the same thing, and set up a road block on the roads leading from the airport to the capital to catch travellers, intimidate them and ask them for what is known in Nigeria as "dash"; a bribe or a fee to continue your journey. The local police turned a blind eye to these activities.

The next day I had arranged a meeting with Mr Coker, the Nigerian based solicitor who was representing Baker Perkins in the case. I walked from the hotel to central Lagos and had a look round at the colourful markets and street theatre. The solicitors' office was an imposing former colonial building just off the main square. I went in and was ushered into Mr Coker's office. He was a very tall, well-built man, wearing a western suit, with a resonating deep voice and English accent, having been educated at an English public school and then Oxford. He reassured me that all was under control and we should get judgement in our favour at the Court Hearing tomorrow. Just before I left the meeting, I asked Mr Coker if I could use his toilet. He said, "Of course", handed me a key and pointed me in the direction I needed to go, which was through the back office area where his clerks and support staff were located. As I passed through this area, there were five or six people, all men, sitting at their desks but slumped forward, having an afternoon nap. Nobody considered this unusual and obviously the 'Lagos Siesta' was standard practice in prestigious law offices in the capital.

The next day I attended at the Supreme Court of Lagos State but the judge was ill and the case was adjourned for fifty-six days. The continual Court adjournments for no particular reason was a common feature in this particular case and, to my colleagues and the E.C.G.D. back in England, these delays were unacceptable. In Lagos, this was the way legal proceedings were conducted and in the five years I was at Baker Perkins, I do not think this case was ever resolved. It was just given the "Lagos adjournment" each time the case came to Court. Some back in England suspected that the other party we were suing were using "dash" to bribe Court officials but Mr Coker just laughed at this suggestion. I am not sure whether he laughed because he believed it was true or because it was a ridiculous suggestion.

The next day, it was time to get back home. Billy took me back to the airport with no road block problems but I had about £200 worth of naira, the local Nigerian currency, and it was a criminal offence to take this money out of the country without official written permission. There were four or five foreign exchange booths; all except one were closed due to lack of funds. I pushed to the front of the scrum of people at the open booth and explained to the cashier that I wanted English pounds – none, dollars – none, did they have anything else? She held up a five guilder note. Yes, that would be fine - guilders. No, I did not understand. She only had one five guilder note; that was all she had. I thought quickly and decided to take the risk of taking the currency out with me and back to the UK. However, as I went through passport control and customs, I was searched and I was given the choice of being arrested or allowing the customs officials to "confiscate" the £200 worth of naira. I took the second option and surprisingly there was no paperwork to sign. I finally got on the British Airways flight, very relieved to be going home.

When I got back to the office, I was contacted by a man named Graham Coveyduck, who explained to me that he had been referred to us via E.C.G.D. and his father had been a senior police officer in Lagos in colonial days and he was effective in working his way around the difficulties that existed in enforcing contracts and recovering money in Lagos. He was off to Lagos in the next few days and we agreed to meet on his return. I heard nothing further from Mr Coveyduck until I was flicking through The Times newspaper one day and there was a report of a British citizen, called Graham Coveyduck, being held in a Lagos "hellhole" prison without charge or trial and questions had been asked in the House of Commons as to what efforts were being made diplomatically to secure his release. He had been in prison for twelve months and obviously had been far too successful and caused problems for prominent local people who dealt with the problem in their own way. Having a case in the Supreme Court of Lagos was a very different experience for me with interesting lessons in geography, culture, and court procedures.

Not many lawyers qualified to practice in England have the opportunity to travel outside the country to ply their trade and whilst as company solicitor at Baker Perkins, I did have the opportunity to travel to exotic places like Lagos, Nigeria. I also pursued claims on behalf of the company in the courts of Luxembourg, the Netherlands, Italy and Greece and had to travel to and liaise with local lawyers in these countries. In my experience business travel was not particularly glamorous or exciting. It usually involved hanging around an airport and then as soon as the flight arrived at the destination, getting into a taxi and off to a hotel with a nice meal in the evening, a meeting the next day and then back to the airport and home. However, I was to experience another very unusual and exotic destination.

At the beginning of 1988, Baker Perkins began negotiating the sale of their business to a large multinational American conglomerate called Rockwell Corporation. They already had quite a substantial base in the United Kingdom and I knew that if I stayed with the company, the legal side of the business would be dealt with from the Rockwell head office in London. This would mean that I would have to commute with a two hour journey each way, relocate to nearer London or look for another job. I knew a lot of people in the Peterborough area and had already built up my own private conveyancing practice acting for friends, relatives and work colleagues. In anticipation of changes which would be forced upon me, I decided to resign from my safe, secure, pensionable employment with private health insurance and a company car and set off on the journey of self-employment with all the inherent risks of uncertainty. Therefore, on the 1 May 1988, I started my high street solicitors practice known as Roger Terrell & Co Solicitors. I was faced with the daunting task of moving from dealing with multimillion pound supply contracts for a public quoted company to dealing with everyday conveyancing transactions, divorces and petty criminal matters from wherever I could get work. It led me to take on some unusual cases as we shall see.

Friday night was always boys night out. After a hard week, me, my brother-in-law Paul and a group of friends would go round the pubs, have a few drinks and always end up at the Shah Jehan Indian Restaurant in Park Road, Peterborough. The restaurant was very busy and lively and we got to know the owners and waiters well. As always, when people get to know you are a lawyer they come up with a legal problem which they would like some help on. A Friday night, after a few pints and a chicken madras, is not the ideal time so when my good friend and waiter, Ishaq Qureshi, asked me about an immigration problem his nephew, Jehanzeb, was experiencing, I asked him to come into the office. Ishaq had always said to me, "You must come to Pakistan, you would love it." After a few drinks on a Friday I was up for anything and would have agreed to a trip to the moon if it had been on the agenda. When Ishaq came into the office he told me he was not joking; he wanted me to go to Pakistan and visit the British High Commission in Islamabad to sort out this immigration problem. He had booked the flights; we would go for seven nights and stay at his house in his village, near the town of Sarai Alamgir, in the Punjab. All the arrangements were put in place very quickly and a couple of weeks later we flew out on Pakistan International Airlines. As our flight took off from Heathrow, I was thinking, "What am I doing?" Not plying my trade in the local County Court but off to the British High Commission in Islamabad to represent a client. I was certain not many English lawyers had had that "privilege" to date. The immediate problem I encountered was on the outward flight. We were in a non-smoking area but fifty percent of the passengers were smoking. I pointed this out to a stewardess and she just said "yes" and everybody carried on smoking for the whole flight regardless. Eventually we landed at a chaotic Islamabad airport and were met by Ishaq's relatives and taken on an hour and a half drive to their village in the Punjab. The Pakistani people are very friendly and hospitable and always make you welcome and make sure you have a drink and food to eat. Ishaq and I were looked after well by his relatives and we had trips out to Lahore and the Mangla Dam and into Mirpur in Azad Kashmir to meet the Chief Justice of Azad Kashmir and other legal dignitaries. This meeting had been set up via a friend in Peterborough who was well-established in Kashmir.

The next day we went off to the British High Commission in Islamabad and reported to the desk and sat down; waiting, waiting and waiting. After about two hours an official came to the counter. He had the file for the relative of Ishaq we wished to discuss. They told me the problem. We had the information with us that they required and we provided it to the official. He was very non-committal and would not give any indication as to how long the application would take, just a "leave it with us". There was nothing more we could do and were pleased with the progress we had made.

That night, to celebrate, Ishaq told me we were staying in Rawalpindi and we were going to have a night out to celebrate our successful meeting. Ishaq's cousin was a solicitor and another close relative was a senior police officer in Rawalpindi and they would show us the sights. We went out to the main commercial area of Rawalpindi and then through some back streets. We stopped for a drink - Lhasi; no lager! We were chatting, laughing and joking. I did not really know where we were going and I did not like to ask. Eventually, we came to a large three storey house and knocked on the door. The heavy wooden door creaked open and there was a middle-aged lady standing there and behind her I could see seven or eight young and attractive girls, dressed in traditional costume. My heart sank and I was thinking, "What is this place? I am here in a very alien environment, a long way from home." "What hospitality am I going to be offered and, if it is what I think it is, can I turn it down without causing offence?" All four of us were ushered into the house and up some stairs to a back room, where the four or five local business men who had been there got out quickly when they were told by the police officer in our group that it was a police raid. We then took their places sitting on the floor and marsala tea was brought into us. Ishaq then gave me a wad of local money with low denomination notes. The music started up and into the room came five or six dancing girls. I quickly caught on that as they danced you threw money towards them for their entertainment. To my relief they kept their clothes on and there were no other "services" offered. A bit different, but this was a boys' night out in Pakistan!

In my experience, everybody that I have spoken to who has visited Pakistan, even if they are originally from Pakistan, has had stomach problems. I do not know enough about the subject but I believe it is something to do with the bacteria in the water. I do not know the causes but I certainly know the effects; violent vomiting, diarrhoea and stomach pains and a desire just to lie down and sleep. Just as I could feel these symptoms coming on, we had been invited to an engagement party for Ishaq's nephew, Ahmed. I knew Ahmed from Peterborough and he was getting engaged to a young lady from the next village near Jhellum. I managed to get dressed and get in the car to the party venue. I could hardly speak and could not move, except to use the toilet. I had to be polite but I was just not in the party mood and very pleased when we got back to Ishaq's house in his village.

The next morning I got up and was feeling a little better and thought a shower would really freshen me up and make me feel good. I went to the bathroom, got in the nice hot shower, lathered and shampooed myself up and then simultaneously there was a power cut and a water cut. There I was, in a village in the middle of the Punjab with the after effects of food poisoning, naked, covered in soap and shampoo, with no idea when or if my situation was to improve! Luckily, after a few minutes, which seemed like hours, the water and power came back on and I was able to finish my shower and I did then feel much better although I was looking forward to going home the next day.

We did not do much that day but Ishaq asked me if he could pack some presents in my suitcase as he did not have enough room in his case and he had some things he had to take back to England as he had made promises to people. Now, Ishaq is a really good friend; he has never been in trouble and would do anything for me but I was nervous. His brother, Younis, who unfortunately has now passed away, was known in the local Pakistani community with the well-known nickname of "Younis Crook". He was convicted of people, alcohol and drug smuggling and served time in prison. I was sure any doubts I had were totally unfounded and Ishaq had been so hospitable to me that I could not refuse his request. However, I thought to myself, "If I get stopped going through customs back at Heathrow, I will explain before they open my case that I did not pack it." I was worried.

In any event, the next day our cases were packed and we headed off to the airport for our Pakistan International Airlines flight home. We had the same routine with the no smoking area but arrived back and collected our luggage and started our long walk towards customs. I was ready with my plan but as so often, there were no officers in the customs area and we just sailed through. We got picked up and went to Ishaq's house first to open the suitcases. True to his word, there were just a few presents for his family. What a fuss about nothing!

Very few English people visit the remote villages in the Punjab and Azad Kashmir and the Pakistani community really appreciated the fact that I had taken the time and trouble to visit their homeland. As a result, I have been a bit of a legend amongst the Peterborough taxi drivers of Pakistani origin as, "Mr Roger, the lawyer who went to Pakistan."

3. *The Italian Job Mark I and II*

Peterborough has a large well-respected, well-established Italian community which arose when the London Brick Company invited Italian workers from the Avellino area of Southern Italy to come over to England and work in the brickyards in the 1950s and 1960s. The men came and brought their families and stayed. They are lovely, hospitable people with great restaurants but they do have a tendency to fall out amongst themselves and within families.

A good friend and client of mine, Pasquale, said he had a legal problem he wanted to discuss. He came to see me and explained that in approximately 1982, his widowed mother had married a man from Italy and they had purchased a house together in Clarence Road, Peterborough. Unfortunately, more or less as soon as they were married they both realised they had made a mistake. He said he was going back to Italy, which he did, and told her to do what she wanted with the house. She did not want to live on her own and now six years on from her husband leaving, she too wanted to return to Italy and sell her share in the house. I went to look at the house and it was a derelict, inner-terraced house in a street of Victorian terraced houses. In reasonable condition it was probably worth about £7,000. Pasquale asked me whether I wanted to buy his mother's half share. No, I did not. A one half share in a derelict house with the other half owned by some untraceable estranged husband living in Italy was not an attractive proposition. Pasquale said, "Just pay anything, she cannot sell it and her husband said he just wanted it to fall down." I thought about it. The state the house was in was causing the City Council concern as they were getting complaints from neighbours and there was a possibility they would take out a compulsory purchase order to solve the problem. I told Pasquale I would pay £1,000 and his mother signed the transfer and she escaped back into happiness in Italy.

Whilst I was thinking what to do with my "investment", I arranged for my carpenter brother-in-law Paul to make the property secure as there were stories it had been occupied by squatters. Paul and I turned up, went to the rear of the property, and Paul kicked the door in. When we walked in, the house was in a terrible state and there was evidence of recent occupation with lager cans and cider bottles everywhere. Paul then went upstairs and I followed him. He went into the main bedroom but suddenly turned around and pushed by me down the stairs and out of the house. I followed and once we were out, I shouted to Paul and said, "Why are we running?" He said there was an old tramp in the bedroom who had threatened him with a broken bottle. We had a rethink and decided to come back in a couple of days and board the house up, which is what we did, but fortunately when we returned the house was empty and there were no problems in making it secure.

I then decided to make my own enquiries of the Italian community to see if anyone knew where the estranged husband was in Italy. I had the number for "Carmine", a local car dealer who was a nephew of the husband. I explained that I was now a half-owner of the property and did his uncle want to sell his half? I would give him £2,000. A few days later Carmine came back and said that as his uncle's wife no longer owned her half he would be prepared to sell his half, but I would have to take the money to a town called Cecina, just south of Pisa in Italy. No problems. I prepared all the legal documents, got a banker's draft for £2,000 in lira and arranged a meeting at a lawyer's office in Cecina. I organised an interpreter and booked the flights for the interpreter, my wife and myself to Pisa. We flew on the Tuesday, had a look around the Leaning Tower, then went onto Cecina, handed over the money and got the transfer deed signed and witnessed. All done. I must be the first solicitor who has purchased a Victorian terraced house in Clarence Road, Peterborough by travelling to Cecina in Italy. I got the title registered into my name, got a local authority refurbishment grant and let the property out for several years. Everybody was happy.

A while later in March 1997, I got involved with another case involving a member of the Peterborough Italian community. This time the circumstances were much more distressing and urgent. Lisa and her husband originally came from a small village called Carosino, near Taranto, in Southern Italy. Lisa had family in Peterborough and she, her husband and their young daughter, Melania, moved to Peterborough. Unfortunately, the relationship broke down. Thankfully the parties got on well and organised between themselves regular contact for the father with Melania on Saturdays. Melania was three years old.

Then, one Saturday in March, the nightmare began for Lisa. The father took Melania for a contact visit and did not return. Lisa was beside herself with worry and telephoned and visited everybody she could think of who might have information, without success. She went to the police and they told her this was a civil matter and no crime had been committed and she must consult a solicitor. I saw her on the Monday and, understandably, she was inconsolable and really worried about where her daughter was and she suspected the worst; that her husband had taken Melania to Italy. We had to act swiftly and immediately. I made an application to the Peterborough County Court for a Residence Order, which was granted. By this time, Melania and her father had been spotted back in the Carosino village in Italy.

Now we knew where they were we could take some action. There is an agreement between certain countries, including England and Italy, to enforce court orders in relation to children, where a child has been abducted. This agreement is called the Hague Convention. We registered our Order with the Lord Chancellor's Office in London and this trigged the Hague Convention procedures. Generally, all court procedures are slow and time consuming and cases are often adjourned or delayed. This against a background of worry and anguish for a young mother being unlawfully separated from her young daughter. Surprisingly, the Hague Convention procedures worked well and the Lord Chancellor's office liaised well with the local legal system in Italy and a court hearing was soon set up and the father had to attend court and explain his position. The Italian court quite rightly took the view that however good and genuine the motives of the husband were, his actions could not be justified and the court ordered that Melania should be reunited with her mother back in England.

Lisa immediately travelled to Italy and collected her daughter from her reluctant husband and then mother and daughter joyfully travelled back to England to be received by a huge family party and celebration. The whole procedure took about three months. As more and more people from overseas and couples from different ethnic and religious groups intermarry, have children and separate the issue of where the parties and in particular the children live has become much more of an issue, particularly where one party takes the law into their own hands and returns to the country from which they originally came. Not all countries are signatories to the Hague Convention and many countries have completely different criteria to the English Courts in deciding where children live. We often read horror stories in the newspapers where children have been abducted by one of their parents and taken abroad not to be seen by the other parent for years. Unfortunately, this may be an increasing trend but at least our story had a happy ending.

4. Marriages, Divorces and Finances

My client was the cheeky, chirpy, Jack-the-lad cockney who had moved up to Peterborough from the East End of London for cheaper housing and more opportunities to develop his French polishing business, which his family had been involved in for generations. We will call him Dave. He lived in the Bretton area of the city and his mum, dad and two brothers all lived close by. I was just finishing off his divorce from his first "trouble and strife" and he had found new love and happiness very close to home; his next door neighbour. She was a lovely Scouse lady, with a large family, all locally based, including mother, father and three sisters. Dave came into the office with the new love of his life on the Friday to pick up his Decree Absolute. He had arranged his wedding for the Saturday at 11am at the Register Office on Thorpe Road and the plan was to then go back to the two homes in Bretton for an all-day reception with both families equally represented and raring to go; the husband's mainly male cockneys and the wife's mainly female scousers. I wished them good luck and hoped they had a good day.

On the Monday, following the wedding, Dave unexpectedly rang me. I enquired how the wedding and reception went and he told me the wedding was fine but the reception was a disaster. Straight from the wedding at 11.00am, all the friends and relatives had gone back to the houses in Bretton, which they had made "open houses." There was food and alcohol laid out in both houses and throughout the day and into the evening the guests moved freely between the two "open" houses mingling, eating and gradually getting merrier and merrier.

At about 11.00pm, after a good twelve hours partying, one of the cockney boys said something to one of the scouse girls, or it may have been the other way round, nobody could really remember, and all hell let loose. Each family reverted to family loyalties and the police had to be called to separate the warring factions. This resulted in Dave spending his wedding night, not with his new wife, but in the cells at Thorpe Wood Police Station, charged with common assault on his new wife and one of his new sisters-in-law. His brother, the best man at the wedding, was also being charged with common assault on one of the other sisters-in-law, who had been one of the bridesmaids at the wedding earlier in the day. What a complete mess. The case was due to be dealt with at Peterborough Magistrates' Court the following Thursday.

I duly attended court on the Thursday and there had been some wheeler-dealing behind the scenes and the new wife and her sisters had told the police and the Crown Prosecution Service that they no longer wished to pursue their complaints and the two families were reconciled. The Court, police and Crown Prosecution Service were not happy because of the amount of time and expense taken up by the complaints but, reluctantly, the Court discontinued the cases. The Court is a public court and the story got out via an agency to either The People or The News of the World, where it made headlines the following Sunday. A very unusual way of getting wedding photographs in the newspapers but I do believe, although the marriage got off to a bad start, the parties are still happily married.

★

Weddings are always joyous occasions. They are where every community and every family shows off a little but hopefully everyone has a really good, memorable day for all the right reasons, with good food, plenty to drink and entertainment for all. Mr and Mrs Smith consulted me about their wedding about a month after the event. They and their guests would never forget the wedding and reception. It was memorable for all the wrong reasons. They had a traditional white wedding at Yaxley Parish Church and then off to a well-known hotel in Peterborough City Centre for their reception, including a carved buffet.

The wedding, reception and carved buffet all went well and the happy couple were to spend the night in the wedding suite at the hotel. Unfortunately, by the time the majority of the guests had given them their best wishes, the bride and groom were feeling decidedly ill with the early signs of food poisoning. The remainder of the guests left and the bride and groom went up to the honeymoon suite, unfortunately both unable to consummate their marriage but both very able to continually be using the bathroom facilities.

The next day they were both very ill and had to cancel their honeymoon and spent the next seven to ten days ill in bed with food poisoning. Another fifteen to twenty guests also complained of symptoms of varying degrees and the Environmental Health Department of Peterborough City Council were called in to investigate. They took statements from all the guests and some samples from some of them and they traced the problem back to the turkey being served as part of the carved buffet. The hotel was prosecuted.

We were then faced with the task of pursuing claims for compensation on behalf of the bride and groom, best man, proud parents and other guests against the insurers of the hotel. I will ask the question but everybody will have their own view – what monetary value do you put on a bride and groom not being able to enjoy their wedding night? In any event, we managed to negotiate fairly substantial settlements on behalf of all the claimants as one thing was for sure - the hotel did not want any publicity whatsoever relating to the disastrous day.

★

Divorce and relationship breakdowns are subjects which fascinate many people, particularly the high profile marriage break-ups, such as the cases of Sir Paul McCartney and the Prince and Princess of Wales. Eastenders and Coronation Street have also featured plenty of cases of conflict between couples. Unfortunately, the reality of everyday life is that many ordinary people also become involved in the stress, trauma and conflict of relationship breakdowns and find themselves in our offices seeking legal advice on divorce. There are a number of myths that surround the law in this area which originate in and are enforced by television and films, often from America. Clients have all sorts of misconceptions as to the reasons they wish to put forward for the breakdown of their relationships but under English Law, there is only one ground for divorce, i.e. the irretrievable breakdown of the marriage evidenced by one of five grounds; the other party's adultery, the other party's unreasonable behaviour, two years separation and both parties consenting, two years desertion and lastly, five years separation. Unfortunately, for an immediate divorce, a party must prove the other party's adultery or unreasonable behaviour. This is potentially a very confrontational system, which does little to promote good relations between the parties, particularly when there are children and financial issues to be resolved. Some legal systems, such as Australia, just provide for the parties to have lived separately and apart for one year. This seems to be a much better system as there is no need for confrontation and unpleasant allegations, which are usually denied by the other party. There are very few contested divorces as if one party wants out of a marriage; there is little point in the other party contesting it.

Proving adultery is a subject which concerns many clients. The easiest and most effective way of proving adultery, which is as we all know, a married person having consensual sex with a person who they are not married to, is by that party's signed admission called "a confession statement". Usually parties providing a confession statement insist that the adultery only took place after the marriage had broken down for other reasons. Whether this is true or not, this explanation seems to give comfort and an excuse for the behaviour. In the past, if evidence could not be obtained by an admission, an enquiry agent would be instructed at considerable cost to follow the adulterous pair to a house or hotel room and observe their behaviour from afar. A report would then be filed with the Court asking the Judge to draw conclusions from the behaviour detected. This procedure is no longer necessary and if adultery cannot be proved by admission, there is usually enough unreasonable behaviour around to substantiate a divorce. As far as proof of adultery is concerned, I did have one distraught client who came into see me with a Tesco carrier bag full of soiled tissues. He was a gentleman originally from Southern Italy and clearly he was very upset. He explained to me that, "My wifa commita adultery in my bed witha my besta frienda." When I asked him how he knew he tipped out on my desk the tissues from his Tesco bag and told me that the tissues were from the scene of the crime and could be tested for DNA. I thanked him very much for the potential evidence but I told him we could write to his wife and ask for an admission and that we did not need to keep the tissues on a file but if he kept them safely as he had promised, we could have them if we needed them. Thankfully we did not need his DNA evidence!

★

On occasions we have had clients contact us for what is a very unusual application, not for divorce but for a nullity, which is really asserting that a valid marriage never took place. A young lady from the local travelling community contacted us and came in to see me with her sister as support. Their first language was Romany and they spoke in this language between themselves. I had never heard this language before. The client explained to me that she had met this young man, also from the travelling community, and she had got on with him reasonably well and been out with him on a few occasions. One evening his mood suddenly changed and he told her they were getting married and she had no choice but to agree and he punched her and threatened her. He bundled her into his car and drove to Leicester where they slept in the car overnight. He then took her to a Register Office the next day and with the help of his friends as witnesses, they went through a marriage ceremony. He must have somehow previously given the required notices. The "happy" couple then went back to his car and after a couple of hours she managed to escape and return to her family. This was a very, very unusual case and the client did go to the police but they were not interested and said it was a civil matter between the parties. Again, as usual they said no criminal offence had taken place. We got the case together and obtained a nullity decree for the client because due to the force and threats against her the marriage was not consensual. We have also had one occasion where the person our client was marrying was still married to his first wife, as his divorce had not been finalised. He had either given a false declaration or falsified his Decree Absolute. The client subsequently found out two years later and contacted his ex-wife and the police. By this time her "husband" was in Canada and the local police did not consider the crime to be serious enough for any further action. The client got her nullity decree.

★

Lawyers often joke amongst themselves that the case is only as good as the client. If the case has a good result the client will say it was because it was a good case and you could not lose but if you do get a bad result usually, in the client's view that is totally down to the lawyer. However, there are some areas of law where the Court and the Court Rules provide for the client to give full and frank disclosure. The main area where these disclosure rules apply is in relation to financial disclosure between husband and wife in financial proceedings arising from the breakdown of a marriage.

Some clients see this disclosure requirement very much like an extension of the requirements of the Inland Revenue and they see it very much as an opportunity to be vague, evasive and creative about their financial position and the demands of their ex-partner.

Dennis, a self-employed car dealer, fell exactly into this category. He had got hold of £200,000 from the sale of matrimonial property in his sole name and in three months all the money had been spent, according to Dennis. As is standard practice, I explained to Dennis there needed to be receipts for all expenditure where possible and an audit trail showing the money passing through bank accounts and being linked to assets which had been acquired. Unfortunately, Dennis was not good with paperwork and dealt almost exclusively in cash.

The headlines of where the £200,000 had gone were;

Gambling	£10,000
Holidays and weekend breaks away	£30,000
Laser treatment for eyes	£4,000

Golf clubs, trolley, bays	£10,000
Men's Rolex watch	£13,000
Ladies' Rolex watch	£10,000
Other jewellery and luxury items	£20,000
Repayment of a loan to a friend from the travelling community	£25,000

The theme of the expenditure followed the above pattern and I was charged with recording this information in writing to present to the District Judge at a hearing at Peterborough County Court coming up in the next few days. I warned Dennis about the rules of full and frank disclosure and that the District Judge would not be happy but he insisted that he had told me the truth and said it may be difficult to believe but he was down and depressed by the breakdown of his marriage and spending all the matrimonial money was his way of dealing with this problem.

We turned up at Court on the appointed day. The solicitors for Dennis' wife and the court had previously received a copy of the financial statement made by Dennis, detailing how the matrimonial money had been spent. Outside the court, the solicitor handed me a Questionnaire for Dennis to complete requiring him to give dates, amounts, receipts, valuations etc to support all the expenditure claimed. Very little of this information was available. Dennis and myself and his wife and her solicitor went into the court room. The District Judge looked over his glasses, and addressed me on behalf of Dennis. "Mr Terrell, it is impossible for your client to have spent £200,000 in three months in the circumstances that he sets out. Your client is wearing a Rolex watch and a ring, are these items he purchased from the monies?" "Yes sir" I replied. "Tell him to take them off and hand them here to me." Dennis duly obliged and I handed the Rolex watch and the gold ring to the judge. "These items will be held in the court safe until further order," the judge sternly told Dennis. "What about these other items, where are they?" the judge asked. I explained that some of the items were at his home and under his control. The judge then specified these items - golf clubs, jewellery, expensive luggage - and ordered that they should be delivered to the wife's solicitor's office by 4pm the following day. The judge also ordered that a Penal Notice be endorsed on the Order of the court. This meant that if Dennis did not comply with the Order without an extremely good excuse, he would be committed to prison until such time as he did comply. I did explain to the judge that Dennis had also purchased some expensive Hugo Boss underwear, one item of which he was wearing and if the judge thought it appropriate, he would also deposit this underwear with the court. On reflection, I do not know what possessed me to say this to the judge but he certainly did not see the funny side of my comments and made that clear to me in no uncertain terms. The judge ordered us out of court. We were taken aback by the hostile reaction of the judge but he made it clear, in no uncertain terms, that he wanted such assets as existed to be preserved and for a full explanation as to the remainder of the expenditure.

Dennis and I discussed the situation and although he and his wife were getting divorced, they had children together and they got on reasonably well. They decided to have a chat without lawyers present to see if they could resolve matters between themselves. Bearing in mind the fright Dennis had received from the judge, he suddenly decided he could borrow some money from friends and relatives. After about half an hour Dennis and his wife came out of their meeting, both with beaming smiles. Surprise, surprise, they had managed to reach a cash settlement. They were both happy and the matter would be resolved by payment of a cash sum to the wife within twenty-eight days. Everybody was happy and Dennis avoided the threat of a spell at Her Majesty's Pleasure. Sometimes, judges are very helpful in shaking cases up and making people see reason, after being given a little encouragement!

★

It is often said that Britain is a nation of animal lovers. Most families, particularly with young children, have a pet from time to time. In the past it was dogs, cats, rabbits and hamsters but now it is probably more exotic birds, reptiles, pot bellied pigs, tarantulas; the list is endless. In some families the looking after of the "pet" becomes a way of life and a very expensive hobby, particularly where there are horses involved. Unfortunately, parties become very emotionally attached to their pets, and in rare cases, obsessive. Therefore, when relationships break down the pet becomes an issue and the question of who is going to have "custody" of Polly the Parrott or Butch the Dog has to be answered. Although it may upset some pet lovers to hear this, as far as the law is concerned, the family pet is a possession and they are dealt with by the courts in the same way as the parties' television, fridge and settee. This is not an easy area in practical terms as possessions are often of low or little value but parties can become entrenched and unreasonable when it comes to dividing them up.

I have been involved in a number of cases when a particular horse or horses have to be professionally valued and that valuation is added to the parties' assets to be divided up by the judge at the final financial hearing relating to the division of assets in the breakdown of a marriage. Not long ago I was involved in a case where the parakeet was particularly dear to both parties. They had separated but the bird, called "Tommy," was in the care and control of the husband in its cage in the former matrimonial home. After lengthy discussions the husband agreed that he would hand Tommy over to his ex-partner. No problem at this stage but the ex-wife did not want her ex-husband to know her whereabouts and therefore, she did not want to disclose her address to him. The ex-husband's barrister informed me that his client would be quite happy to deliver the bird in its cage to our office and we could then make arrangements direct with our client for her to collect it. I thought about this proposal for a moment. What if the bird was delivered to us and it died whilst it was in our care and control before our client could collect it? What if the receptionist caught bird flu? There seemed far too many pitfalls but luckily our client came up with a venue for the handover at a mutually trusted friend's house and my anxiety was therefore overcome.

Only a few weeks later I got involved in another bird case, this time a parrot, and again at a court hearing before a District Judge to either agree by negotiation a division of the assets, or if not agreed, the matter would have to be listed for a hearing and for the parties to give oral evidence on the financial dispute between them. I do not think I was ever told the name of the parrot but I will call it "Polly." Both parties had provided, as is required by the court rules, details of their assets, liabilities, income, pensions etc. The husband was representing himself and was, unusually in such circumstances, being quite cooperative and polite. I was representing the wife. Both parties had worked at Royal Mail and the husband had quite a substantial pension. The negotiations went on for a while and the subject of a Pension Sharing Order came up. My client then said to me, "Tell him he can keep his pension if he lets me have Polly." Up until this stage we had been involved in intense and serious negotiations trying to resolve important financial issues and this proposal was completely out of context and I just impulsively laughed. I know I should not have done this and I should have taken the suggestion seriously and to laugh was totally unprofessional of me. The reaction of the client? She burst into tears and sobbed, "You do not know what that parrot means to me." Clearly I did not and I apologised and went off to discuss the matter with the husband. Before I put the proposal to him about leaving his pension intact if we could have the parrot, I asked him where the parrot was. Clearly, there had been previous discussions between the parties and he immediately replied, "It's gone, I've given it away, and it's gone to a home for parrots." I reported this back to my client and she was devastated and told me that she did not believe her ex-husband but she finally accepted there was very little we could do and we resumed financial discussions without mention of the parrot. It later occurred to me that we could have suggested that we find another parrot of the opposite sex and get the parrots to breed and then the client and her ex-husband could have a parrot each. I thought about this a little further and decided that perhaps it was best just to leave the parrot situation as it was and let sleeping dogs lie.

5. *Shell Shock, Dealing with the Paparazzi and a Show Case*

Barry Daniels was a middle-aged married man and a manager at Le Maitre Fireworks Ltd, who operated in the Fengate area of Peterborough. They produced fireworks on a commercial scale for large pyrotechnic displays and celebrations, such as New Year, and had a national and international reputation for their work. Unfortunately, for those concerned, the commercial production of fireworks is an extremely hazardous process and is the nearest thing to a wartime munitions factory. On a late September morning, Barry was working on some papers in his office and his colleagues on the adjacent shop floor, including a Michael Darroch, were pressing gun powder into seven pound display fireworks. One of these fireworks exploded. The explosion ripped through the wood and corrugated iron building and blew the unfortunate Michael Darroch through the roof, killing him instantly. Barry came rushing out of his office, took charge of setting off alarms and evacuating the premises and called the emergency services. He searched in the debris for Michael and eventually found his body which had suffered horrific injuries. Although he had no physical injuries, these events had a profound psychological effect on Barry and he had some time off. He returned to work but despite his requests for more time off to try and come to terms with what had happened, these requests were refused by his employers. Eight months after the accident he was dismissed and did not work again.

He eventually consulted the old established firm of solicitors in Lincoln Road, Peterborough called Jeffreys, Orrell & Co, where I had previously done some work experience, and they initiated a claim on his behalf. I took over this firm in March 1995 and at the back of one of the filing cabinets of the litigation partner, I found Barry's file, which had had little or no attention for some months. I immediately contacted Barry and went to see him and his disabled wife at his bungalow in the Dogsthorpe area of Peterborough. He was clearly down and depressed and did not want to go ahead with the case. The insurers of Le Maitre Fireworks denied liability at every level; he had not witnessed the death of his work colleague, only the aftermath, and it was not foreseeable that he would suffer the grave psychological reaction that he did suffer. He was not even particularly close to the scene of the explosion. Both myself and his wife Brenda tried to encourage him to press on with the case. His claim would be contested at every stage but he had been psychologically damaged by the negligence of Le Maitre and he was entitled to damages. Eventually, he agreed and we pressed on, dealing with the filing of statements, medical evidence, claims and defence. The matter was then listed for a fourteen day contested hearing before Mrs Justice Steel sitting at the Royal Courts of Justice in The Strand.

For a person of normal fortitude, the High Court is a daunting experience. It looks, from the inside and the outside, very much like a gothic cathedral and is the height of Victorian grandeur. Whilst the building itself is grand, it is populated by hundreds of barristers in their wigs and flowing gowns, all rushing around and looking extremely important and knowing exactly what they are doing.

Into this environment came Barry, his disabled wife, whom he was pushing in a wheelchair and myself as his legal team. We located our barrister, Mr McRowland, and after a brief conference our case was called on at 10.30am. The court rooms in the Royal Courts are oak panelled and the Judge sits at a bench or a raised platform, very much like the traditional image we have of a court room. The barristers representing the parties are in their wigs and gowns and there is still a real air of formality and importance in the venue and the way the proceedings are presented to the court by the barristers.

Barry was the first witness called to give evidence and he very slowly and carefully told the hushed Court in a quiet voice exactly what happened on the day of the accident. He now suffered from temper rages and lack of concentration and he found it impossible to carry out the simplest of tasks. Here we were, seven years after the accident and he was a virtual recluse. Barry's version of his psychological problems was supported by a consultant psychologist from the Maudsley Hospital, a world renowned establishment for the treatment of Barry's condition, known as Post Traumatic Stress Disorder. This was the condition that first became apparent in soldiers who served in the trenches in the First World War and it was then known as "shell shock." Le Maitre's barrister gave Barry a hard time in cross-examination, suggesting that he was already suffering from the symptoms that he was complaining were caused by the explosion and that he was exaggerating and just trying to get compensation. They called their own expert medical evidence that contradicted our evidence. They also called witnesses who tried to assert that Barry was not close or friendly with the deceased Mr Darroch.

Mrs Justice Steel had a very difficult task weighing up the contradictory versions and evidence generally over the fourteen days of the Trial. Despite the tenacious defence set up by Le Maitre, the judge found in favour of Barry and awarded him over £200,000 in compensation. He and his wife were vindicated and all the time, trouble and delays had been worthwhile. The psychological condition Barry was suffering from made it impossible to conduct interviews with the journalists or appear before the TV cameras waiting outside on the steps of the court. He asked me to do the interviews and I just kept matters very simple and expressed his thanks to those who had supported him and explained that he and his wife just wanted to be left alone. He just wanted to get home to his bungalow as quickly as he could. I did keep in touch with him for a while but unfortunately his wife died and he moved away to the Norfolk coast. The compensation did not improve Barry's life and he was the same as all people I have acted for who have received compensation. He said to me, "Thanks Roger, but I would give all the compensation back to be as I was before the accident." I am sure he meant exactly what he said.

★

It was lunchtime on a really lovely early summer's day in June and my colleague, Nassar Khalil, arrived back to the office from representing one of his clients who was held in custody at Thorpe Wood Police Station in Peterborough. For us to be representing clients at the Police Station was a regular occurrence. However, over the previous weekend, the IRA had carried out a bombing at the Arndale Centre in Central Manchester. The explosion had caused huge material destruction but even worse had injured two hundred innocent people. The nation was outraged and the story was the lead for all news programmes and the headlines in the all the newspapers. The hunt was on for the IRA bombers and their accomplices. What was the connection? How did the activities of the IRA involve us? Nassar told me that when he went into the Police Station and when he came out, there was a huge group of reporters and journalists stopping him and asking him if it was his client who had been arrested. Who was this man? Had he been charged? Apparently, a man from the Peterborough area was being questioned at Thorpe Wood Police Station by Manchester Police and Special Branch officers in connection with the IRA bombing in Manchester. He had been held for ten hours. Nassar correctly denied all knowledge of the person being detained but the journalists would not have it and they said they knew we were acting and what was going on. Clearly, they were under pressure from their editors to get a story. The telephone then started ringing at the office with journalists from all the major national newspapers and the BBC, ITV and Sky wanting to do interviews with us. The problem was that we did not represent the person who was being detained. Whilst Nassar had been at the station he had got hold of the name of the person who had been arrested: Shabir Khan. He, like Nassar, was a member of the large but close-knit Peterborough Pakistani community. Nassar said he would get hold of him and see what all the fuss was about. Nassar made a few telephone calls and made arrangements for me and him to go and see Mr Khan, who by this time had been released without charge by the police and Special Branch.

We went to Mr Khan's house in the Millfield area of Peterborough. He told us that he did not have a solicitor and he was quite happy for us to represent him. He explained that he was a taxi driver. At about 11.40am on the previous Friday, he had been waiting at the taxi rank outside Tesco's in Broadway, Peterborough. He was approached by a man, who he described as thirty-five to forty years old; about five feet eight inches tall, heavy build, round face and short brown hair with an Irish accent. He asked Mr Khan to take a package to a travellers' site at Eye near Peterborough and deliver it. He gave him £5.00 for the fare. Mr Khan had been asked to deliver packages before and thought nothing of it, carried out the task and got on with his job as normal. It later transpired that the package contained £2,000 in cash, which was to pay for a Ford cargo lorry. This was later collected from a yard in Fengate, Peterborough by an unknown person but now known to be acting on behalf of the IRA, driven up to Manchester, packed with home-made explosives, parked in the Arndale Centre in Central Manchester and subsequently detonated, causing massive destruction and injury. After the explosion, police enquiries led to the taxi firm and then to the driver, Mr Khan, who was detained and questioned, initially as a suspect, although it soon become clear his involvement was innocent and that he was a witness and not part of an IRA terrorist cell. Although this was exciting stuff and the case was hot news, Mr Khan did not really have any need for solicitors and he was, of course, not going to be charged with any offences. However, because of the media frenzy, he did have a story to sell and we could help him do that.

Before we could even attempt to sell his story, we had to make sure that this would not prejudice the police/Special Branch enquiry and, more particularly, would not expose Mr Khan or his family to the possibly of threats and intimidation from sources connected to the IRA. We therefore met at Thorpe Wood with the Special Branch officers leading the investigation and explained to these very ordinary looking young men that Mr Khan was proposing to sell his story to a national Sunday newspaper (they paid the best money) and would this cause a problem? They confirmed that as far as they were concerned, selling the story would not inhibit their investigation and that there had never been a case of witness intimidation by the IRA where witnesses were based on mainland Britain. We also thought that it was hard enough for us to find Mr Khan, knowing people and living in Peterborough ourselves, so this would have been an added problem for the IRA had they come looking for him.

This was the first time I had been involved in selling a story to a Sunday tabloid – not an easy task! They all want to know what the story is in detail, who else you have spoken to and what they are offering. The danger is that if you give too much away they have got the story for nothing or they can spoil the story you have sold to their rivals. The other major fact is that the story is only hot for a few days and then is superseded by the next breaking story. Eventually, we sold the story to The People for a five figure sum and signed their contract. Mr Khan did the interview with their reporter in our offices and they took photographs of him in his taxi at the scene where he had collected the money. The theme of the story was that he had seen the face of the IRA. The story was to be published the following Sunday.

On the Friday night, the sub-editor called me and said they had changed their mind and were not sure if they were going to run the story. They would guarantee running it if our client accepted a fee reduced by fifty percent of that stated in the contract. The contract did state that publication was subject to the discretion of the Editor and the five figure publication was only payable on publication. I went mad and ranted and raved and threatened to sue but in reality they had been clever and I had been foolish. They relented and published the story and paid the fee originally agreed. However, it was a very good experience for me to understand how difficult it is to deal in the cut throat world of the national media even before phone hacking!

★

It was late in the afternoon on the day before Christmas Eve. The office was very quiet as a lot of the staff were off dealing with their last minute Christmas shopping. My phone rang and the receptionist told me that Chris, the manager of the local Showcase Cinema at Fengate, Peterborough was on the line. I immediately thought, "Why on earth would he be ringing just before Christmas?" Anyway, "Put him through" I said. He introduced himself and explained that the Christmas and New Year holiday period was their busiest time of the year. However, early that morning, thirty caravans from members of the travelling community had driven on to his car park and one of their members had told him that they would be staying until the New Year. He had the latest Hollywood blockbuster opening on New Year's Day and expected record attendances but as things stood at the moment, the car parking arrangements would be very limited. He had been onto his head office but their usual solicitors were not available and they suggested he try a local firm.

He had rung five firms and I was the last on his list. "Could you help?" I was trying to think quickly, whilst Chris was outlining the problem. Had I ever previously acted for a client to evict illegal squatters from their land? No. Was I familiar with this area of law and the procedures involved? No. Was it only one working day before a major bank holiday when all offices, courts etc would be closed? Yes. The reality was that my quick risk assessment very quickly led me to the conclusion that I, in common with all the other lawyers contacted by Chris so far, did not want this job. I did not have the heart to tell Chris I did not want the job however. Therefore I thought of a figure the job was worth and then doubled it on the assumption that Chris would politely decline on the basis that the proposed fee was too much. I gave him the figure and he said he had no idea whether it was acceptable and would ring his head office. Five minutes later, he rang me back and said, "Fine, let's go ahead." I had got the job from hell which nobody wanted. I spent the rest of the day researching the law, taking a full statement from Chris and preparing the application to the Court. I arranged a hearing for us the next day at 10.00am at Peterborough County Court before District Judge Wharton. The dreaded day arrived and at 10.00am on 24 December, Chris and I appeared before District Judge Wharton. He carefully read through the application for an order evicting the trespassers from the Showcase Cinema car park and the statement by Chris setting out the facts. He felt that the case had been made out but the person or persons unknown who were the Respondents, i.e. the members of the travelling community parked on the Showcase Cinema car park, should have notice of the hearing and the proposed orders to be made so they had the opportunity to be heard and make representations if they so chose before the Court made any decisions. He therefore directed that Chris and I should attend the Showcase Cinema car park within the next hour and affix to lampposts or other prominent areas at least six copies of the Court Order and a notice that the matter would be heard later that day at 4.00pm and any parties wishing to attend the court should do so. Chris and I thanked the Judge and waited for a few minutes for the Court Order to be typed and sealed and then headed for the Showcase Cinema. On arrival at the Showcase Cinema we went into Chris's office and equipped ourselves with sellotape and scissors and stepped out into the vast car park and headed towards the bottom corner, where the travellers' vans were parked. As we made our way across the expanse of tarmac, a pack of what must have been fifteen dogs headed towards us. They were all sizes and all breeds from big lurcher-type dogs barking and snapping to small terriers yapping and trying to bite our heels. We carried on regardless and managed to get most of the Court Notices displayed. The dogs continued to harass us but then a group of seven or eight young children appeared and asked us what we were doing and told us how we were wasting our time. Finally, an elderly, tall gentleman came out from one of the caravans and identified himself as one of the leaders and elders of the group. We handed him a Court Notice and explained to him that if he wished to say anything to the judge he should be at court at 4.00pm that day. He was very polite and told us that as a group they kept getting moved on and that they would not be staying long and would move off on New Year's Day. Now a little muddier, colder and bitten around the ankles, we had got the Notices served in accordance with the judge's Order and Chris and I were back before him at 4:00pm and explained what had happened. Nobody from the travelling community showed up, the Judge was satisfied that the correct procedures had been followed and made the Eviction Order. As we waited for the court staff to type up and seal the Order, we realised we had only done about fifty percent of what was required, as we still had to enforce the Order and get the caravans off the car park.

Chris and I went straight down to Thorpe Wood Police Station and spoke with the appropriate officer. The private bailiffs we would instruct would not act without police back-up as they were worried about the potential reaction from the travellers. Because of the holiday season and staff shortages, notwithstanding that the Court Order said possession forthwith, the police could not get the appropriately trained team of officers together until the morning of 1 January, some seven days later. We argued and complained but nothing could be done. Early on the morning of 1 January, thirty police officers arrived in their vans with full protective gear, riot shields, batons etc, to be met with the thirty travellers' caravans voluntarily leaving the car park as they said they would be doing. The Hollywood blockbuster opened later in the day and there was no hindrance to any of their customers using the car park. I got my fee and Chris also gave me and my family complimentary tickets for any show for the next three months. Everybody was happy!

6. Murder in Middlemarch

It was Saturday morning and I had awoken a little late. I had been out on the Friday night and had had a couple of drinks too many. I was not feeling my normal perky self. My wife Cherry was up and had got breakfast on the table. She was waiting for me to come downstairs. When I walked into the kitchen, she was sitting at the table reading the Daily Mail. She did not say, "Good morning" or "How do you feel?" she just looked down at the open newspaper and pointed to an article. She said, "It's definitely the husband." She handed me the paper and I started to read the two page story headed, "Murder in Middlemarch" by Paul Bracchi and Ben Taylor. The story outlined that Mark Williams and his wife Sarah were recently both married for a second time. They lived in a luxury home, called Stable House, in a tranquil, idyllic village called Upton, near an ancient market town in Lincolnshire. The town had been the setting for the BBC series, Middlemarch and I shall call it Middlemarch.

What had happened at the luxury home a couple of weeks earlier is almost too hideous to imagine. Sarah's body was found floating, fully clothed, in the swimming pool. She had been attacked in her kitchen where there were traces of blood. A tap in the sink was still running when the police arrived and a bottle of washing up liquid lay on the floor where it had fallen. Detectives believed she was still alive, although unconscious, when her body was dragged outside and thrown into the swimming pool. The body of Sarah's cat, Cleo, was also floating in the pool beside her. The scene belonged in a crime novel or film but not here with the rows of quaint stone-built houses with names like Thimble Cottage and where the local pub had a thatched roof and stood amid a sea of rolling farmland, hedgerows, lush meadows and leafy woodland. The article described the couple as having an extravagant and enviable lifestyle with expensive vehicles with personalised number plates. Sarah owned a beauty salon in Middlemarch and they both went jet-skiing at weekends at a nearby lakeside resort where they owned a weekend retreat. The only visible sign that this tranquillity had been shattered was a police car parked outside Stable House and a poster appealing for information about the murder on the village notice board. The article then posed the question everybody was asking, "Who killed Sarah and why?" There was then some speculation. The police had more or less ruled out a burglary that had gone wrong and were quoted as saying, "It is very rare in Lincolnshire to be attacked by a stranger in your own home." According to the article, Mark Williams had been living in rented accommodation in Peterborough and working part-time selling furniture and selling and recycling second hand books. The couple were living lives of millionaires but where did their money come from? The police were investigating Mr Williams' business links as a matter of routine. The journalists had contacted a business associate of Mr Williams called Joe Azzopardi or "Maltese Joe" as he was known locally. He had a penchant for gold jewellery and every Saturday he could be found selling behind a well-stocked table of books at the market in Market Square in Middlemarch. A local resident was quoted as saying, "To be perfectly honest, I do not think anyone really knew what Mark Williams did and how he made his money. He was just a wheeler-dealer." It was also revealed that on the night of the murder, Mark Williams and Joe Azzopardi were in Amsterdam. If the murderer was not a stranger, who was the killer? Did Sarah know her attacker or was it a professional killer? The article concluded by saying that eighteen days after the terrible events at Stable House, Sarah's killer was still at large, the reason for her death remained a mystery and an atmosphere of suspicion and disbelief hung over the village where they had lived.

The publicity the case was receiving on the television, radio and in newspapers, both locally and nationally was getting the local communities talking and speculating, and indeed it was the main topic of conversation in our office on the following Monday. One of my former colleagues, a solicitor called Nassar Khalil, telephoned me that morning and asked if I was acting for Mark Williams as he had acted for him on his divorce from his first wife whilst he had worked for me. I told him that I had heard nothing from anyone about the murder other than what I had heard and read in the media.

On the Wednesday afternoon, I had a couple of appointments at 3.00pm and 4.00pm but I was not particularly busy. I had been very kindly invited by a professional footballer friend called Gary Breen to attend a European Nations Cup qualifier between the Republic of Ireland and Turkey at Landsdowne Road, Dublin on the Saturday. Gary had been a player at Peterborough United and had moved on to Coventry City in the Premier League. He was now an established international footballer for the Republic of Ireland. I had remained friendly with him as his career progressed and he always instructed me if he needed any legal work carried out. He had invited me and my son Edward, who was fifteen at the time, to the game. Gary was very kindly paying for the flights and the hotel and Edward and I were really looking forward to it.

At just past 2.00pm, Sharon, our receptionist, came rushing upstairs to my office from reception and said, "It's him, that man, the murder at Upton, he's in reception and he wants to see you." I asked her to slow down and she clarified that Mark Williams was in the office without an appointment and could I see him? I went straight downstairs, introduced myself to him and went into an interview room. Mark was well over six feet tall and well-built. He was later described by a number of people as a heavier George Michael look-alike. Mark and I both agreed that was a fair description. He briefly explained to me what had happened, which was very similar to the content of the Daily Mail article which I had read on the Saturday. In particular, he had been in Amsterdam with Joe Azzopardi at the time of the murder and had rushed straight home. He was upset and he had made a full and detailed statement to the police regarding his movements at the relevant time. As far as he knew, Joe Azzopardi had also made a statement, as had Mark's brother, Neil Williams, and Mark's friend, David Beech. Mark had seen David Beech at the police station. I explained to Mark that it was standard police procedure to take very full and detailed statements from persons close to the deceased to check their timings of when and where they were and whether any witnesses could corroborate their movements. I told Mark that although it was clearly a very difficult time for him, if he told the police the truth he would have nothing to worry about. Mark agreed that there could be no evidence against him as he was not involved in Sarah's death but he believed and feared the police had some information they were not telling him about and he was going to be arrested.

As an experienced criminal lawyer, I was fully aware that if the police had any suspicions about Mark Williams' involvement in his wife's death, they would have to arrest him, caution him, question him in the presence of a lawyer and put to him whatever evidence they had that, in their view, implicated him in the murder. I gave Mark my business card and told him to call me immediately if he was arrested or, if he was not allowed to call, to get the custody sergeant at whatever police station he was at to call and I would attend with him immediately, whatever time of day and whatever else I was doing at the time.

Mark was understandably clearly upset and worried but he took my business card and left the office to go to his father's house in Peterborough. He had been staying with his father as Stable House was a crime scene and was being examined by the police forensic team in detail for over a week or so. A few days later the property was handed back to Mark with a twist, which we were later to discover.

Late on the Thursday afternoon, I received the anticipated telephone call from the custody sergeant at Spalding Police Station, telling me that my client Mark Williams had been arrested by Lincolnshire Police and he was being conveyed to Boston Police Station where he would be held and questioned on an allegation that he had murdered his wife, Sarah Williams. I later found out that earlier that day they had arrested another man from Peterborough, David Beech, in connection with the murder and he was being held at Spalding Police Station. The national media immediately ran the story and David Beech was named and described in The Sun and The Daily Mail as aged thirty years, one of Mr Williams' best friends and best man at his wedding nine years earlier to his first wife. They had been friends for twelve years, having met at the Baker Perkins engineering firm in Peterborough.

As the police had arrested Mark late in the day and taken him to Boston, they were not going to question him until the Friday morning. I spoke to Mark on the telephone at Boston Police Station and told him this and explained that we would have a chance to discuss matters in detail before any police interviews took place.

I did not sleep particularly well that night. I was thinking that the police must have some substantial evidence. To arrest someone on suspicion of murder in a very high profile case is not action they would take lightly or without very good reasons. All sorts of things were going through my mind. Was Mark telling the truth? Had he come back from Amsterdam earlier? What evidence had the police got? Were there any witnesses who had implicated Mark?

In the morning I went into the office and got together some notebooks. I had no papers at all relating to the case at this stage and as I drove over to Boston, which is about a one hour drive from Peterborough, the same questions were going through my mind. When I arrived at the police station, I went through the normal booking in procedures with the custody sergeant and then asked to see Mark in private to discuss our tactics in what was to be a crucial forty-eight hours.

Friends and acquaintances often ask me when they know I have acted for clients charged or arrested on suspicion of a serious criminal act, "How can you represent them when you know they are guilty?" The answer to that question is very simple. Under English law a person is innocent until proved guilty. This is a principle established centuries ago, probably in the Magna Carta, but it is still a basic rule of English criminal law. Therefore, if an accuser, now the police in modern times, asserts that a person has committed a criminal offence, they must prove the commission of that offence "beyond reasonable doubt." Usually, lawyers will say that is about ninety-five percent, unlike civil matters where the standard of proof is on "the balance of probabilities" which is about fifty-one percent. Basically, this means that the prosecution must be able to show by producing properly and legally obtained evidence that the accused committed the crime without any real doubt. It must be remembered that it is not for the person accused to show anything or answer any allegations in any way. He can go through an interview in the police station and merely answer every question put to him, "No comment." The court cannot draw any adverse inferences from this unless he later comes up with a version of events which he should have disclosed in the police station, i.e. an alibi. In serious crimes, such as murder, it is a jury; twelve ordinary people on the electoral roll, who decide the fate of the accused person after hearing the evidence, the cross-examination, the submissions by barristers and the directions and summing up of the Trial Judge.

Therefore, not knowing anything about the police case and not knowing how Mark was or what he would say, I sat in the interview room at Boston Police Station and Mark was ushered in, sat down and the door was shut. Now, Mark Williams was a very confident, intelligent man and was used to negotiating and discussing uncomfortable matters; in actual fact, an ideal client to represent in a police station. I went through with him the terms of the police caution, explained that he could do a "no comment" interview if he wished and asked him whether his version of events that he gave me in my office a couple of days earlier was still the same. He said it was still the same and that he had no problems answering any police questions and he had no reason not to fully co-operate. I told him that I believed the two police officers who would interview him would do a "tough cop/soft cop" routine, with one officer being aggressive and accusing and the other officer trying to be friendly and reason with him. Before I spoke with the police officers, I asked Mark again, had he told me everything? He told me he had.

I then spoke to the two senior experienced detective constables from Lincolnshire Constabulary. They gave me a copy of the original witness statement Mark had given to them and they told me they wished to put to him some of what they considered to be inconsistencies in that statement. I also knew that there was a team of detectives working on the case. They had trawled through Mark's businesses, interviewed his friends, associates and acquaintances and had been checking on Mark's recent movements with the help of

CCTV where possible. As one would expect, it later became clear that they had done a very thorough job. I went back to see Mark and showed him his statement, which he of course remembered and told him what they proposed to do. He was quite relaxed and happy with the situation but I was still thinking to myself, they have no evidence and I said to Mark, that they must have, as I described it, "a rabbit or two to pull out of the hat"; something major that they had not yet disclosed to us. Also, all parties were aware that David Beech had also been arrested on suspicion of the murder. What was he saying? Was he implicating Mark in some way? The answers to these questions would be revealed in the next twenty-four hours.

I told the detective constables we were ready for the interview to begin and they came into the interview room and explained to Mark that the interview was to be taped and that he or his solicitors would be given copies of the tapes. The interview room was not large with just enough room for a large table and bench seats facing each other. On the table was the standard issue tape recording machine upon which the interview would be recorded for the benefit and protection of both parties and, more importantly, for the purposes of evidence if Mark was charged and the matter went to court. I sat next to Mark and the two detectives sat opposite. The detectives and their team had obviously spent a considerable amount of time planning this interview, which was crucial to them establishing any case which could proceed to a prosecution. My role was not to assist Mark in the answering of any questions put to him but to ensure that the questions asked were within the correct admissibility of evidence rules and if Mark was unsure of his position at any time to ask for a short break for a private consultation with me. These procedures and rules have built up over a number of years and have been the subject of Acts of Parliament, Reviews, Royal Commissions etc. Therefore the principles relating to what the police can and cannot do and the inferences drawn from an accused's answers are well established. To be fair to the police, in my experience, they were always scrupulous to make sure the correct procedures were followed and that there could be no suggestion of relevant evidence being obtained by improper means.

Clearly, the police had to think of the possible motive Mark would have for allegedly being involved in the murder of his wife and their questioning would be trying to establish a motive in the first instance and thereafter establish how Mark would be involved in the carrying out of the murder. Detectives are obviously highly trained in techniques of interviewing suspects at the police station. It is a fundamental part of their job. In my experience, they usually start off very friendly and relaxed and try and gain the confidence of the person they are interviewing to get them talking.

The detectives adopted exactly that approach. They asked Mark about how he and Sarah met, where they lived and for how long, what jobs they did and where they went socially; all fairly mundane stuff which Mark could easily answer. Their mood then changed and they started putting to Mark that he and Sarah were not getting on; that they did not go out together socially; that he did not like her appearance; that he was associating with other women and enjoying the services of prostitutes. Mark dealt well and, I believe, truthfully, with all the questions which were asked, although some clearly made him uncomfortable. After two or three hours we had a break and the detectives switched off the tapes and went out of the interview room.

Mark asked me how I thought it had gone. I thought it had gone well and clearly none of the questions that had been put at this stage suggested or implicated Mark in any way in the murder of his wife. I told Mark this and told him yet again that they would be hitting us with something big and unexpected. We knew that whilst they were interviewing Mark, another team of detectives was interviewing David Beech at Spalding Police Station about twenty miles away. Obviously, the two teams of detectives were talking.

We had a break of about fifteen minutes and before we recommenced one of the detectives asked if he could have a word. I agreed and we went into a side room. They told me they had a significant piece of evidence which put a completely different complexion on the case. They had searched David Beech's flat at Stagshaw Drive in Peterborough. At the back of a cupboard, underneath the sink in the kitchen, they had found a letter which David Beech had written to his father. They handed me a photocopy of the handwritten letter and also showed me the original. This is what the letter said:

"Dear Dad, I gather as you are reading this something has happened to me. If for any reason you think my death was innocent, please destroy this and do not read any further. I do not have many requests only that when given the opportunity please control Alex (David Beech's son), I love him to bits but he does lack discipline and a good father figure. I have been nothing other than an w****r with money which has caused me to do this thing I am about to tell you. Please do not mourn me because I do not deserve it, just remember me up to the time I stopped living with you. These days were the best for me. This letter is one of two. Please give the registered recorded letter to the police, unopened. There will be one of three reasons for my death. Number one – natural or accidental death. Number two – a man hates me and has it in his head that I have slept with his girlfriend. Number three – this is probably the real reason for my death. Mark Williams has probably either paid for my hit or killed me himself. Possibly a boat accident, car accident or while on holiday with him or if I started going on business trips on my own where he has an alibi. Mark Williams has known that I have huge debts and has offered me £20,000 to kill Sarah in the pool plus the cat. He will be in London and Amsterdam – perfect alibi. I will come over and get her by the pool and hit her on the head and dump her in the pool to drown. After that I will put the cat in a basket to stop me getting scratched and drown the cat, making it look like Sarah went to find the cat and hit her head as she stumbled by the pool and fell under the cover and drowned. This frees him to have a playboy life, to see Tania and others, the boat in Malta, the house he has paid for, no mortgage, less expense as she spends lots. This will also enable him to sell her business which makes nothing. This is one of his real gripes – that he has to pay for everything. Mark has two businesses both run from his home. We say we used the fibre for animal bedding, actually Mark sells books and card in Spain and Malta for huge profits as well as markets in England – half of the money goes to Millennium Industries and half is cash and cheques to Mark Williams. He is looking to set up a current account in Malta. Major tax evasion, fraud etc. I am really sorry to have let you all down including myself. I am not blaming anybody but myself for what I have done."

I paused for a while and because of the seriousness of the content of the letter, I had to read it over and over again to make sure I understood the content. I believed that there was no doubt that it was a legitimate letter and this was the one and only real piece of evidence, together with David Beech as a witness, that the police were relying on to implicate and to charge Mark. The detectives told me they were going to use the next interview session to question Mark in detail about this letter and its contents. Understandably, they seemed very confident that they had cracked the case. They told me to take as much time as I needed with Mark in private and when we were ready they would recommence the interview.

I went back into the interview room, showed Mark the photocopy letter and told him where it had been found. I recounted to Mark the conversation I had had with the detectives. He was obviously upset, shocked and in disbelief, one, because he now knew that David Beech murdered his wife and, two, because Beech was saying that he only did this because Mark was going to pay him £20,000. I knew that Mark in particular and myself as his lawyer had to try and stay calm and deal with this matter in a sensible, logical way as the replies to the questions Mark was to be asked in the next couple of hours would be crucial to the outcome of the case. Once Mark overcame his initial emotion from knowing who murdered his wife and that it was his best friend, he settled down. Mark told me that the content of the letter was ridiculous and a complete fantasy. There had never been any discussions over the murder of Sarah, payment of £20,000 or any of the other matters alleged in the letter. In addition, as a matter of evidence, although the police were excited by this evidence, as a matter of law it was uncorroborated evidence by one co-accused against the other co-accused and on its own was not strong, unless again there was further evidence the police were not telling us about or if further evidence subsequently came to light. I felt confident that the police had now revealed their hand and it was for Mark and I to deal with it. Mark and I had a further discussion and agreed as before he would truthfully answer the police questions and he did not want to give a "no comment" interview as he had nothing to hide. I told the detectives that Mark was ready to continue with the interview, they came in, sat down, and turned on the tapes.

Both detectives were now very confident and aggressive with the evidence they now had and gave Mark a hard time, alleging that his marriage was over, that he was associating with other women, and that he wanted to get rid of his wife. To divorce her would have cost him too much, so he got his best mate to knock her off and make it look like an accident. After it had all died down, he would pay him £20,000; a perfect result for both conspirators. Mark could have got rid of his wife for £20,000; much less than the cost of a divorce, and David Beech would have money to pay off his debts. Mark, of course, carefully considered all the questions that were put to him, and answered them, denying any knowledge, involvement or conspiracy. By the time this line of questioning had finished it was getting late. The police indicated they did not really have many more, if any, further questions. They told us they would speak to Lincolnshire Crown Prosecution Service and to their senior officers and would let us know what action they would take.

At this stage, the police held all the cards. They probably had enough evidence to charge, although it was just David Beech's evidence. The police officers left the interview room and I discussed the options with Mark. They could release him without charge at this stage, on police bail, pending further enquiries. This would mean that they could have another month or so to gather further evidence and re-interview. I thought this would be unlikely as there was considerable media interest in the case and the police were under pressure to charge. They could charge him with murder or conspiracy to murder. I thought this, unfortunately, would be the option they would go for, with the serious impact and all the implications it would have for Mark.

Bearing in mind I had a commitment I could not miss in Dublin, I organised for Alison Leviesley, a solicitor colleague of mine to come over and meet Mark and the police and be fully briefed for events in Boston Police Station the following day. On the Saturday, my son Edward and I went to Dublin and had a great time around Temple Bar and then went on to the football match which ended in a 1-1 draw. We returned home on the Sunday. I telephoned Alison and she told me that there had only been one major development and it was major – Mark had been charged with murder and conspiracy to murder and had been remanded in custody to appear at Spalding Magistrates' Court on the following Monday.

On the Monday I drove over from my office in Peterborough to Spalding Magistrates' Court, a journey of about twenty-five miles. I was very familiar with the Victorian neo-medieval castle-look Court. The court was swarming with large mobile TV wagons, local and national newspaper reporters and photographers plus sightseers. I pushed through the crowd and reported to the usher. Mark was being held in the cells at the bottom of the building, a bit like a dungeon. I was shown through to him. We had a brief chat. The police had produced no additional evidence and not much was going to happen that day. David Beech was also in the cells and they were going to appear in the dock together for the first time, charged with murder. Mark and Beech were brought up from the cells. The court room was packed and the Magistrates walked in and sat down. The Clerk of the court asked Beech and Mark to confirm their identity and the prosecution solicitor stood up and outlined the prosecution's case to the Magistrates. Beech was in tears. Mark listened intently and shook his head. At this stage in the proceedings it was for the prosecution to provide to us defence lawyers copies of all the statements and other evidence that they wished to rely on to secure a conviction against our clients. Lincolnshire Police had investigated the crime and gathered the evidence. This evidence was then handed over to separate organisation called the Crown Prosecution Service (CPS) who then collate the evidence and provide copies to ourselves. The CPS then instructs the prosecution barristers and deal with the administrative functions regarding the case. Obviously, the police and the CPS work very closely together. The case was adjourned to Middlemarch Magistrates' Court whilst the prosecution prepared their case. Mark was remanded in custody to HM Prison, Nottingham and Beech to HM Prison, Lincoln. The police were very keen to keep Mark and Beech apart as Beech was their star witness in the case against Mark and, in view of the content of the letter Beech had written to his father, they were worried about possible threats made by Mark to Beech which might intimidate him and encourage him not to give evidence or to change his story.

As far as the media are concerned, these early court appearances are a bit of an anti-climax. No evidence is given and the information revealed by the prosecution is already in the public domain. Therefore, they have to try and obtain some sort of story to make their attendance worthwhile. I gave a quote to the media which I had agreed with Mark beforehand: "He looks forward to the opportunity to present his version of events to the court in due course. He is in good spirits and very positive." The media all ran with stories showing photographs of Mark and Beech at Mark's first wedding where Beech was best man and of Mark and Sarah at their wedding, with Beech standing next to them, headed "Picture of Wedding Joy."

Whilst the prosecution were preparing their case in readiness for the parties to be committed for trial at the Crown Court, there were a number of developments. Always when acting for a person charged with the most serious crime – murder – the cause of death of the deceased is important to establish. The police pathologist had carried out a post mortem and the cause of death was drowning, although the poor lady had substantial head injuries caused by a blunt object and an attempt had been made to strangle her. A post mortem was also carried out on Cleo, the cat found dead in the pool with Sarah. This revealed the cat had also died from drowning. It is usual for defence lawyers to obtain their own post mortem if there is any doubt as to the cause of death. We considered this was important as Mark was not at the scene of the crime and Beech had admitted the killing but had not yet pleaded guilty. In the event, the pathologist we instructed carried out a post mortem and came to the same conclusions as to the cause of death. Sarah's body could then be released for her funeral. We must never forget that Sarah was a totally innocent and respectable person who had been subjected to a terrible ordeal. She was laid to rest in December. Mark wanted to attend the funeral but the prison authorities would not allow it. Instead, his brother Neil attended on his behalf. Ironically, five days later the prison authorities allowed Mark an escorted visit to Scunthorpe to pay his respects at Sarah's grave.

The Lincolnshire CPS then made a terrible error regarding the police case and their evidence. By virtue of an administrative mistake, we were sent lengthy transcripts of tape recordings made at the murder scene, Stable House. Immediately after the murder, Stable House was a crime scene and thoroughly examined by the police forensic team for possible evidence which would link potential suspects to the crime. After this forensic work had been completed, the police "bugged" Mark's living room, kitchen and a couple of other rooms with listening devices. They then allowed Mark to return to the property. They could then listen in on Mark's conversations with whoever else was in the house, which was usually his brother Neil. Now, this is very common practice by the police and it is not illegal, provided the correct procedures are followed. The content of these tape recordings are not admissible in evidence before the court but the listening devices are installed by the police to try and establish what potential accused persons are discussing or planning, e.g. "We will meet at a certain time and place to dispose of some initial piece of evidence or discuss what has happened." The reality of these tapes I am sure was very disappointing for the police as the main discussions between Mark and his brother Neil was whether they should have a Chinese takeaway or a pizza and whether they should watch the football or the boxing! The disclosure of this evidence was a basic error and revealed to us the tactics the police were adopting to try and obtain further evidence to assist their case. I understand that the unfortunate person at Lincolnshire CPS who sent the information to us in error was dismissed.

A fundamental issue in the case at this stage was the strength of the prosecution evidence. They only had the letter and Beech's oral evidence. No statements by Beech had been disclosed to us. We wanted to flush their evidence out at an early stage. This evidence, at the latest, had to be available at the committal stage and would usually be provided by way of written statements which set out a prima facie case for the accused person to answer at a Crown Court trial. However, in cases such as this, where the evidence was perceived to be weak, there was also an opportunity for what is called "an old style committal." This is where the relevant witnesses give oral evidence, submissions are then made by the prosecution and defence lawyers and the Magistrates consider this evidence and consider whether there is a prima facie case to answer. The advantage for the defence team is that it is a much better way of testing the strength, quantity and quality of the evidence and the demeanour of the witnesses. It is also a process which is unpopular for the CPS for the reasons above and also because the process is lengthy in time and resources.

We were due in the Middlemarch Magistrates' Court towards the end of January. Middlemarch Magistrates' Court is one of a number of gorgeous Georgian limestone buildings in the town, also used in part as the Town Hall. I remember turning up on one occasion when Colditz had been filmed and the Magistrates' Court was the Gestapo headquarters and a day later the building was bedecked with swastika flags but the business was dealing with the more mundane criminals of South Lincolnshire. The cells in Middlemarch Magistrates' Court were rarely used. They were down some rickety steps in the basement and they certainly looked like the original Georgian set-up. To make matters worse, Mark had been playing badminton with a fellow inmate whilst in prison, fallen awkwardly and injured his leg and he was in plaster with crutches.

It was a real ordeal for Mark to get from the cells up to the court room. The court room was packed with representatives of the media and spectators just interested to see what was going on. Human nature gives us a morbid fascination with persons accused of serious crimes. For some reason we expect them to have an unusual physical appearance and demeanour. Unfortunately, this is not the case and most such people look very ordinary, as did the George Michael lookalike. We indicated to the court that we were going to have an old style committal and the papers would need to be prepared. We also explained that we would be making an application for bail on Mark's behalf. The prosecution were not happy. Outside the court was a huge throng of onlookers to see Mark and Beech arrive and leave by a side door.

In the meantime I visited Mark on remand in prison in Nottingham and we were quietly confident that the case and evidence were under our control and that we were well placed to deal with the case against Mark. However, this quiet confidence was soon to change dramatically. Delivered to our office was a series of boxes containing material on sheets of A4 paper which the prosecution were intending to rely upon in securing the conviction of Mark for murder. Much of it was mundane statements from police officers concerning statements they had taken and interviews they had carried out but amongst these voluminous papers were three statements from a witness named John Bond.

Understandably, the majority of the public are not familiar with the workings, hierarchy and politics inside a prison. Mark was befriended by a fellow inmate called John Bond. Bond had a string of previous convictions including one for perjury (lying under oath) which involved a civil case over debts. He had the role in Nottingham prison of "a listener." He gave informal advice to fellow prisoners and helped them fill in forms and write letters. Bond had made statements to the police alleging that Mark had asked him for help with preparing his case. Bond had then changed the subject and asked Mark about the murder. He said Mark had told him it had been planned for four months and he was to pay Beech £20,000. He went on to state that Mark had an aerial photograph of Stable House which had been printed in newspapers and he had stuck this photograph on the wall of his cell. Bond said Mark was more interested in the house than his wife. Mark also allegedly told Bond that his wife did not support his business ventures and was negative to his ideas. The statements recorded that Bond went back to his cell and made notes of the conversations with Mark in his diary. These statements were a substantial blow to Mark's case. Whatever the truth of them, they added to the strength of the police evidence and we had to abandon our application for an old style committal and our application for bail. However, as we later revealed at the Trial, there was a lot more to John Bond than we knew at this stage. I spoke to Mark about Bond's evidence and he totally rejected the conversations ever took place and told me that Bond was a liar and fantasist. The information he revealed could easily have been gleaned from the newspaper coverage of the case.

The prosecution are under a legal duty to deliver to the defence solicitors copies of all the statements, documents, reports etc upon which they may wish to rely at the Trial. This procedure gives the defence team the opportunity to consider the strength of the evidence, the witnesses and how to approach presenting a case on behalf of an accused person. The prosecution also have to give the defence solicitors the opportunity to look at what is known as "unused material." This material is the statements and other documents obtained by the police in connection with the investigation but which is not considered relevant or significant by the prosecution in establishing the guilt of the accused person. The prosecution, as is standard practice, sent us copies of their unused material and this information revealed how thorough and professional the police had been in investigating the case, the witness statements they had taken and the video tapes they had examined from fixed C.C.T.V cameras monitoring traffic flows. It is amazing how much of our everyday lives are caught on C.C.T.V. Clearly, at one point the police had explored the possibility that the alibi that Mark had given was false and he had driven back to his home on the night of the murder, carried out the crime and then returned to his alibi. Clearly, this did not happen and I did feel sorry for the poor police officer who had to trawl through hours of C.C.T.V showing cars travelling along a road near the scene of the crime.

As part of my preparation of the defence case, I felt it was important for me to visit the scene of the crime to establish the layout of the property and the geography of the kitchen where the murder took place to the swimming pool where the unfortunate lady's body was found. To make arrangements to visit, I had to liaise with the detective investigating the case. They know that I am doing my job and I know that they are doing their job and therefore, there is a mutual respect and understanding which helps such arrangements to take place smoothly without any need for confrontation or awkwardness. On the day in question I was due to be at the property at 10.00am. It was a bright sunny winter's morning and there had been an overnight frost as I walked up the long gravel drive leading up to the front door. I could not help thinking of the poor lady who had been murdered and the ordeal she must have gone through. As I walked into the kitchen, although it had been cleared up, there were still blood stains apparent and the horror of that evening really hit home. Outside the birds were singing and the garden was surprisingly neat and there was the swimming pool where the victim ended up. From a defence lawyer viewpoint, the visit helped me get clear in my own mind the layout and the geography of the house and where the serious events had taken place.

We had now received all the statements and documents containing the prosecution's case and we attended Middlemarch Magistrates' Court again for the formal committal of Mark and Beech for trial at Lincoln Crown Court with a preliminary hearing date of 25 February. In the meantime, we instructed a very impressive barrister named Alex Milne from Red Lion Court Chambers in London to represent Mark at the preliminary Crown Court hearings and the eventual trial.

Lincoln Crown Court is situated in a building called The Castle, adjacent to the magnificent Lincoln Cathedral, which towers over the city. Again, the media were out in force on the day the case first came before the Crown Court and they were to be treated to a sensational performance by David Beech. For once, Mark was the support act.

The Court assembled, the Judge came into the court room and everybody stood up. Beech was in the dock on his own. Mark was to be dealt with separately. The defence and prosecuting barristers were ready for action and the public gallery was packed. The clerk asked Beech to stand and he identified himself by giving his full name and date of birth. He was dressed very smartly in a dark blue suit and tie and wearing glasses. The clerk put to Beech, "That on a date between 19 October and 22 October, you murdered Sarah Williams contrary to common law. How do you plead?" "Guilty" came back his reply, almost choking on his words, as there was a huge gasp of astonishment coming from the people in the public gallery. He also pleaded guilty to the conspiracy to murder charge. The prosecution barrister stood up and outlined the circumstances of the murder to the court. Beech held his head in his hands throughout the hearing and openly sobbed. Asked by His Honour Judge Richard Hutchinson if he knew what was happening, Beech replied, "I do understand." The judge remanded Beech back into the custody of HM Prison Lincoln to be sentenced at a later date. Mark appeared before the judge in the afternoon and entered a "not guilty" plea. His case was adjourned to a date to be fixed. Although as far as the media and prosecutor were concerned, the case would now go quiet until the day of the Trial, we had a mountain of evidence to trawl through and take Mark's instructions upon and we had to select and instruct a senior barrister, known as a Queen's Counsel (QC), to conduct the Trial.

Mark had throughout been remanded to HM Prison Nottingham and Beech to HM Prison Lincoln. They were to be kept separate and apart, as previously mentioned, to avoid any suggestion of collusion or intimidation, particularly now as Beech was the main prosecution witness against Mark. Whilst the police and CPS had teams of detectives, lawyers and administrative staff working on the case, the defence had me and a couple of trainee solicitors. Nottingham Prison is about a one and a half hour drive from my office in Peterborough. It is in Basford, about three miles out of the city centre, on a hill, a very grey looking originally Victorian building with a modern extension and obviously a very high wall all around. The visiting times, even for legal visits, was quite restricted. The prison is Category A and holds persons convicted of the most serious crimes such as robbery, murder, drug dealing, rape etc and also unconvicted persons on remand such as Mark charged with serious offences. Legal visits must be pre-booked and people attending must have identification. The prison staff then allow you into a waiting area which is locked behind you. Once locked, another door opposite is unlocked into another locked holding area, after passing through a metal detector. Once through this area, officers escort you to a general consultation area which includes legal and family visits and has a tea and snack bar. Visits were limited to two hours between 10.00am to 12.00pm, but you could return in the afternoon between 2.00pm and 4.00pm. I had to attend once or twice per week to make sure I had been through all the evidence and received Mark's instructions on all the witnesses we intended to call. In the afternoons, because of family visits and staff shortages, the process could be very slow and tedious. The prison officers, although just doing a job, did try to be polite and cheerful and I remember on one particular slow afternoon the prison officer in charge said to me, "Are you all right?" I said, "Yes thanks, fine." In reality, I was really bored and frustrated with the delays. He then said, "Are your mum and dad all right?" I was rather taken aback and thought he was taking customer care a bit far. He then said, "You do not remember me do you? I'm Chris Parkinson, I used to be your best mate at junior school." As soon as he said it, I realised who he was. I just did not expect to meet him in prison. He said that once I had finished with my client I should come and have a cup of tea with him in his office and we could have a chat. I did and we spent a good hour sharing reminiscences.

As a result of my discussions with Mark, we had to trace and interview potential witnesses including a number of inmates and former inmates who had come across John Bond and who could confirm how unreliable he was. It also came to light that John Bond was being used by the prison authorities and the police to win the confidence of persons charged but not yet convicted and get a confession from them in return for an improvement in his position and a reduction of his sentence.

We also had the problem of finding a top quality QC who would be available for the Trial. The problem with the top people is that they are usually booked months in advance for trials. We already had a very able and competent junior counsel (barrister) in Alex Milne. He suggested a couple of names but they were not available, as did Mark through word of mouth in the prison. We finally came up with a QC named Adrian Fulford and we arranged for him, Mark, Alex Milne and I to have a conference in Nottingham Prison. The prison authorities were very helpful in making time and facilities available but the only interview rooms available which ensure privacy were on the "lifers' wing", i.e. the wing where persons serving life sentences were housed. The appointed day came and I met up with Alex Milne and Adrian Fulford QC at the prison gates and we worked through the necessary procedures to get on to the lifers' wing which was eerily quiet and everything such as locking and unlocking doors and checking in was done really slowly. The other frightening aspect was that this in reality was the place that Mark would be likely to end up were he convicted of murder. Both Adrian Fulford QC and Alex Milne are very impressive characters and very experienced in their field of dealing with persons charged with serious crimes and facing voluminous evidence. The conference lasted about three hours and Mark was very happy at the end and was confident in his team and that he was properly represented and we had every angle covered. Everybody was relieved to be released from the lifers' wing and back into the general prison area and then for Adrian, Alex and I to be back out of the prison gates and back to freedom.

We received the anticipated news a couple of days later that the Trial was due to start at the beginning of July, not at Lincoln Crown Court but at Nottingham Crown Court. The police had received intelligence via the prison network that Mark was paying a hit man either to assassinate Beech before he gave his evidence or to spring Mark from the Lincoln Crown Court as security was not particularly tight. Mark laughed when I told him as he considered both ideas to be ridiculous. As a result of a tremendous amount of time and effort, we were ready for the trial to commence and had our team and witnesses in place.

I drove over to Nottingham on the day of the trial and arrived at 9.00am. Adrian, Alex and I had a meeting with Mark in the cells beneath the court for a last minute briefing and we were ready to go. The media interest was amazing, with all the national newspapers and BBC and ITV present. The public gallery was packed. The judge was His Honour Judge Morland. The prosecution were represented by James Hunt QC. He was an extremely experienced competent barrister with a huge physical presence and a very deep authoritative voice, the nearest thing to Winston Churchill I have heard! Because James Hunt QC says it, it must be true. The police forces in the East Midlands always wanted him to conduct their prosecutions. His record of securing convictions was phenomenal.

In criminal trials of this nature, the jury are sworn in and then the QC for the prosecution opens the case and outlines what evidence the prosecution will call. The prosecution QC uses this opportunity to impress the jury and make the case out at its worst as far as the defence are concerned. James Hunt QC was a master of the opening speech and once he had finished, it looked and sounded as though the only result would be a finding by the jury of guilty and we may as well pack up and go home. It was fantastic oratory. This is how James Hunt QC opened and outlined the case to the jury of eight women and four men, all listening intently: "This case is not a "whodunit" – we know who did it. He has admitted it. It's a "who got him to do it?" This is what this is about and we say it was Williams. Williams had become wealthy through two businesses. One processed cardboard waste and the other involved buying up unsold books which were meant to be shredded into animal bedding. Instead of shredding the books, he sold them in Spain and Malta and at markets across England for a huge profit. He and Sarah lived a lavish lifestyle in Upton near Middlemarch and he ran a powerboat on nearby Tallington Lakes. But Williams was seeing a nutritionist and wanted out of his two year marriage. The relationship was also strained because divorcée Sarah wanted to start a family and Williams, who had two children from his first marriage, did not. Williams had become tired and uninterested in Sarah and was playing with another woman. He had made a lot of money but he wanted his freedom. It would have been expensive to divorce a second wife. She would know too much of his rather shady businesses to be bought off cheaply. He therefore arranged a contract with David Beech to murder Sarah whilst he established his alibi on a supposed business trip. Sarah's body was found in the pool on 20 October, the day after Williams had left for Kent, Essex and Amsterdam. Williams had flown to Holland with associate Joe Azzopardi from Stansted Airport after a night in a hotel in Essex. The alarm was raised when Williams telephoned his brother from Amsterdam to say he could not get any answer from Sarah at home. The post mortem on Sarah revealed she had died from drowning but she had facial injuries, including a broken nose which showed she was probably already unconscious when she went into the water. Police experts found blood stains in the laundry room and kitchen, which indicated she had been attacked inside the house. About £32,000 in cash was found in the house, £31,000 in a bedside cupboard. Although items were disturbed to some extent, it was plain that this was not a burglary. This killing was personal. Beech's fingerprints were found on a Tesco carrier bag containing cash in the master bedroom. A vehicle similar to the Pajero Jeep he drove had also been seen turning into the drive of the house. When questioned, Beech admitted hitting Sarah with a wooden banister post and dumping her body in the pool. He later took police to where he disposed of his bloody clothes, rubber gloves and the post.

In two identical letters addressed to his father before the killing, he revealed Williams' involvement. He revealed that £18,000 cash and the car he used were his if he killed Sarah. This letter to his father read "Mark Williams has offered me £20,000 to kill his wife Sarah. I will come over, get her by the pool, hit her on the head and drag her in the pool to drown. I will then put the cat in the basket to stop me getting scratched and drown it making it look like Sarah went to find the cat."

Azzopardi also told police that Williams had confided in him about the cost of a divorce. He said that he estimated it would cost about £250,000 and admitted that Sarah was the only other person who knew how rich he was. The month before Sarah died, Williams had booked into a health farm in Leicestershire with his mistress, where they had spent a day together in a whirlpool bath and steam room. He told police later they had a "touch and feel" session. David Beech has confessed and will be a witness against Williams who murdered his wife as surely as if he had done it by his own hand."

This was a fantastic summary of the prosecution's case against Mark, intended for the benefit of the judge and jury. It was delivered in a way that was intended to show the case was really strong and would be proved once the witnesses gave their evidence. The national press also had a field day with this very impressive oratory from James Hunt QC. Since the murder and the investigation, charge and initial court appearance at the end of November and the beginning of the new year in January and February, matters had gone quiet and the start of the case was the opportunity to pump up the drama and interest and create anticipation for the next two and a half weeks of the Trial. Mark came into the Court on crutches as he was still suffering from the leg injury he sustained playing badminton when he first went into prison. He listened intently to the evidence and "showed little emotion" according to The Sun newspaper when the two foot pine coloured stair post used to kill Sarah was displayed to the Court, wrapped in clear cellophane.

This is how the press dealt with the headlines on the day after the case opened;

The Daily Telegraph: "Husband paid best man to murder wife." "Businessman feared divorce bill jury told." There were photographs of Sarah and Mark on their wedding day and a separate photograph of David Beech when he was best man at Mark's first wedding. There was also an aerial photograph of Stable House.

The Sun: "Tycoon paid best man to murder his wife. Blonde's body was found in swimming pool. He visited hooker just hours after the killing." There was a photograph of Mark, Sarah and David Beech at Mark and Sarah's wedding, an aerial photograph of Stable House and a photograph of the mistress with whom it was alleged Mark had had a steamy affair.

The Daily Star: "Pal drowned playboy's pretty wife – and the cat – in swimming pool, Court is told" and then in large headlines: "Love-Cheat Hubby paid his best man to bump off bride." There were similar photographs plus a picture of the police forensic team searching Stable House and the Cameo Beauty Parlour run by Sarah in Middlemarch.

The Daily Mirror:The case made the front page of this newspaper with the headline: "Drown her for £20,000 – husband hired best man to kill wife, Court is told." The photographs were the same as in The Sun.

The Daily Mail: "Husband paid me to kill wife." "Best man agreed a £20,000 death deal says QC" was the headline.

The Independent: "Book dealer hired his best man to kill wife."

The national television and regional programmes all ran the story as did the local newspapers and radio stations.

Over the next few days, one by one the prosecution witnesses were called before the Court by James Hunt QC to give evidence. Joe Azzopardi, known as "Maltese Joe", was the first prosecution witness. He was a real character, well known in the Middlemarch area as a local football referee and for selling books on Middlemarch market. I had met Joe years ago and he worked for my uncle as a builder for a while on the construction of my parents' house at

Glatton. I knew he would be perfect for the media. Joe spoke with a strong Maltese accent and on being questioned by James Hunt QC, he described how he and Mark had spent the night when Sarah was killed whilst they were in Amsterdam. He said, "We got to the hotel about 5:00pm and went to see the totty. It was both our idea. It's a nice place to see all the totty." I must admit that the Judge did appear to be nodding off or resting his eyes, but suddenly when Joe mentioned "totty" he came to life and said, "Totty, Mr Azzopardi, what do you mean?" Joe replied, "The girls, the girls." The Judge, jury, all the barristers and the public gallery burst into laughter and the seriousness of the situation was predictably broken by Maltese Joe. Joe went on to say that Mark told him he was going off to see this lady and he was gone for six minutes. James Hunt QC said, "Yes, Mr Azzopardi, when he came back what did you say to him?" Joe replied, "Bloody Nora, you're a fast one." Again, this reply caused the Court room to erupt with laughter. Maltese Joe continued with his evidence and became emotional, held his head in his hands and sobbed when he described how Mark rang him in his room about midnight and told him that Sarah had been murdered.

At the end of the day's evidence, the defence team met with Mark in the cells under the court room to discuss our tactics. The evidence so far proved nothing against Mark but we knew John Bond, his cellmate, was due to give evidence in the next couple of days and Mark wanted me to track down another prisoner he had shared a cell with and who had known John Bond and would discredit him. I checked with the prison authorities and located this prisoner at HM Prison Thorne near Doncaster so I immediately set off to interview him and take a statement.

I went through all the security procedures at HM Prison Thorne and waited in an interview room for my witness to come in, which he did. He was about thirty five years old, normal build with a huge scar along his left cheek about five inches long. He told me he knew Mark and John Bond. Bond was "a listener" and all the inmates knew he was a police informer and he had told this witness that he hoped to get time off his sentence by informing. He said if we got a production order from the Court for him to come to the Trial he would give evidence, which was helpful. I thanked him and he told me that he was serving three years for causing death by dangerous driving and if I was wondering about his scar, this was the punishment meted out to him by an unknown person in Nottingham prison, who slashed him with a razor. He said that it was on behalf of the family of the person killed and he did not make a complaint. This is obviously how things work in the prison system!

The next day, James Hunt QC opened by calling the mistress. The Daily Star called her, "a flame haired beauty" and described how she romped in a jacuzzi with Mark weeks before he allegedly murdered his wife. "Suntanned nutritionist said she kissed and cuddled Mark after booking into a health spa as 'his missus'". She told the court how they had met through David Beech after arranging to buy a set of wardrobes from Mark. Mark later phoned her for advice on fitness and he told her he did not want to start a family with his wife. They kissed for the first time after he took her to a beach where he kept his powerboat and jet ski. When they met again, they went for a walk at a local beauty spot and then went to her home. They eventually went into her bedroom and she admitted there was some intimacy but they did not have sex. She told the Court she was seeing someone else and did not want a full blown affair with a married man.

Other prosecution witnesses called were Mark's first wife, who gave evidence about Mark's reluctance to have children during their marriage and him confiding to her about sleeping with another woman. A friend of Sarah's, called Joanne Hewitt, gave evidence about Sarah wanting to have children and the arguments this caused with Mark. The parties' former housekeeper, Michelle Cook, gave evidence about the marital difficulties between Mark and Sarah. None of the witnesses so far had given any evidence, other than motive and circumstantial evidence to link Mark to the murder and the court and the media knew that the star witness would be David Beech.

Three days into the Trial, David Beech was due to give evidence. When we arrived at court on the day there was a huge armed police presence both inside and outside the court. The police had received a tip off via Nottingham Prison that Mark had organised a hit man to assassinate David Beech before he could give evidence. When I told Mark what was happening he just laughed and felt complimented that the police thought he was capable of organising such "a fantasy."

The court convened and James Hunt QC called David Beech to give his crucial evidence. Wearing glasses and dressed in a blue suit, Beech took the oath and promised on the bible to tell the truth, the whole truth and nothing but the truth. He told the court how he arrived at Stable House at 8.30pm in his white Astra. He had with him a wooden stair post he had bought earlier from a DIY store. Earlier that day he had drowned the cat in the pool as part of a plan to lure the victim outside. The aim was to make it look as if she had tripped trying to save the cat and had fallen in. She was alone, washing up when Beech appeared, and the pair sat down for a coffee. Prosecutor James Hunt QC asked Beech, "Who made the next physical move?" A long silence followed before Beech answered, "I went to get the post and brought it back. Sarah was in the kitchen. She said, "What's that" and "Where did you find it?" I said, "I found it out by the garage." Sarah took a look at it and said, "Put it on the table." I picked it up and hit her with it across the head. I went to pick her up to take her to the pool. There was a lot of blood." Sobbing, he leaned back in the witness box and sat down. "I tried to carry her to the pool. I could not do it. I put my fleece over her head because she was bleeding. It also meant I could not see her." Pressing two fingers over the base of his own throat, Beech showed the Court what he did next. "It's called a sleeper. It is a martial arts expression. If people are conscious when you do that, it makes them unconscious. I tried to pick her up again but I could not do it, she was face down. But as soon as I panicked, I was able to do so. I pushed her to the pool and put her in it." Mr Hunt QC then asked, "How could you do such a thing?" Beech replied, "I had been frightened of him (Williams). I was just doing what he wanted." Beech had been employed by Mark for £30.00 per day to front a business for him. On 8 September the pair had been drinking coffee at Stable House. "He (Williams) took me out to the pool area", recalled Beech. "He said, 'I've got a proposition for you. Twenty grand to knock off Sarah.' I just looked at him. He said, 'I'm being serious. £18,000 and the Astra car to knock off Sarah.'" Beech claimed that Mark then pulled out a photograph from his pocket. "It was a picture of me on holiday ten years ago when I was twenty. It was a holiday I took to Tenerife with Mark. It was a picture of me being raped by two or three guys. I was totally drunk; it was in the early hours of the morning. I had never seen it in my life before. I never knew it existed. My whole world caved in." Beech claimed that Williams threatened to send prints to the mother of Beech's seven year old child, his fiancée and his father. "If I did what he said, I could have it back and the negative," claimed Beech. The photograph was apparently taken by one of Beech's attackers with his own camera and discovered by Mark when he agreed to have the film from the trip developed.

Beech then told the court that after dumping Sarah's body he went back to Stable House to try and clean up and cover his tracks. He added, "It had gone ever so wrong." As he entered the kitchen he was met with the sight of blood splattered walls and large blood stains on the carpet. He said his fleece top, T-shirt, jeans and trainers were covered in blood. He grabbed a tea towel and washing up liquid to try and clean up the mess but he could not remove the stains. He went upstairs where he stripped off his clothes and had a shower before changing into Mark's clothes and stuffing his own into one of Mark's sports bags. He went into the wardrobe in the roof space and took £32,000 cash and then threw other clothes on the floor because he wanted to make the scene look like a burglary. He also collected the bloody wooden murder weapon, a coffee cup from when he and Sarah had chatted earlier in the house, Sarah's purse and several letters from the floor, all of which had been splattered with blood. Beech told the court that several times before he left that night he went back to the pool to see if Sarah had survived but when he saw no water splashes he knew she was dead. Eventually, he got into his car and drove out of the driveway with his lights off, hoping no one would know he had been there. He returned to the murder scene twice more that night with other cleaning materials to cover his tracks. After dumping the murder weapon and other incriminating evidence, he returned to his home in Peterborough. He told the jury, "I just sat and cried in the hallway, looking at myself in the mirror. I was thinking of my whole life and what I had just done."

Earlier, Beech had told the court that he had met Williams when they worked at Baker Perkins in Peterborough and their friendship had continued over the years. He had always confided in Mark. "He has always known who I have been seeing, jobs I have been doing and money matters." He added that, "Mark and Sarah seemed like the perfect couple to the outside world but in private they led separate lives due to Sarah's desire to have children." He said that Mark codenamed his plan "Cleo" after Sarah's cat. However, when he went to Stable House and killed the cat on the afternoon of the murder, Beech said he began to have doubts and telephoned Mark and told him he could not do "Cleo". Mark told him to, "Stop your whingeing and get on with it."

So far all the evidence that Beech had given was in answer to questions that had been asked by James Hunt QC. It was time for our QC, Adrian Fulford, to cross-examine Beech on behalf of Mark. This was probably the most crucial piece of advocacy which would have to be carried out. However, we had also gained evidence via Mark's contacts with fellow inmates from a prisoner called Des Ball. He had been in Lincoln prison with Beech and then moved over to Nottingham and Mark had got to know him. He had given us a crucial statement and Adrian Fulford QC immediately attacked the credibility of Beech's evidence and demeanour. He put it to Beech that Beech had told Des Ball that Beech had been sleeping with Sarah and that she had threatened to tell Mark. Beech also revealed, in cross-examination, that he looked after Stable House for Mark and Sarah whilst they were away on holiday in Malta a few weeks before the murder. During this time, he had sex with his girlfriend on a kitchen table and in Mark's four poster bed and spent two weeks masturbating over porn videos. Beech said he felt he was a spectator to the murder and felt he was having an out of body experience. Mr Fulford QC told Beech he was not asking him these questions to humiliate and embarrass him but, "To illustrate that you did not act like a disturbed man as you claim." At that point the case adjourned for the day.

The following day, Adrian Fulford QC continued with his expert cross-examination of Beech and put it to Beech that he had invented a tissue of wicked lies to implicate Mark in the murder by constantly changing his story when interviewed by the police in October. Mr Fulford QC claimed Beech carried out the murder "coolly and calmly" without expressing any of the hesitation or guilt he claimed was tormenting him at the time. Beech had initially given Mark a glowing character reference and when interviewed by police on 11 November made it clear that the crime was committed alone and there was no involvement from Williams. Mr Fulford QC also expressed disbelief that Beech had never stood up to Williams or ever questioned him about the alleged plot to kill his wife. "Every time he raises it with you, you never once say 'actually this is a bad idea.'" Mr Fulford QC also revealed Beech had at one point told the police that he was in Stable House at the time Sarah was killed and that burglars had bludgeoned her to death, they then left and "you tried to get Sarah to her feet but she would not move." Beech confirmed that this was the third version of events he had given to the police. When it became clear the police had hard evidence linking Beech to the murder, he asked to speak to his solicitor in private and then confessed. Mr Fulford QC then mentioned a statement Beech had given to the police in which he said, "I am not a nice person but neither is she (Sarah). When I saw her bleeding him dry, spending it as quick as he could make it, then I'm sorry but no. Someone who helped me like Mark, no." The police then asked Beech if Williams had wanted rid of his wife and he replied, "Do not put words into my mouth." The letters implicating Mark were then produced to Beech and it was then he made his full confession.

By this time, Beech was into his third day in the witness box and he was showing signs of pressure under the cross-examination and his credibility was in tatters. He told Mr Fulford QC he had not slept for three nights and he did not know what was going through his mind. Taking a deep breath and looking down, he said, "When I killed Sarah I did not know what on earth I was doing. I do not know in what order things happened, right up to it, right after it, times, dates, anything. I just can not remember." The jury was told that in the first three interviews that Beech gave to police he refused to talk about the murder and said "no comment" throughout. Mr Fulford QC stated that Beech had started smirking when police officers showed him a letter found in his flat which gave his reasons why he might be killed. After three days, a very relieved Beech was told he could step down. The jury had listened intently to the contradictory and bizarre answers given by Beech to cross-examination by Mr Fulford QC and looking at the faces of the members of the jury and their demeanour, I just felt the case was moving in favour of Mark.

The next witness called by the prosecution to give evidence was John Bond. Prior to him giving his evidence, there had been consideration and discussions between us in the defence team and the prosecution regarding the admissibility of pages of Bond's evidence. The rules of evidence provide that if a person is to be questioned by police concerning an allegation of crime, the evidence will not be admissible unless a caution, i.e. "You need not say anything etc" is given. As Bond was the agent of the police, the caution should have been given but was not and therefore the majority of Bond's evidence was inadmissible. However, Bond did give some evidence to the so-called cell confession by Mark although its value and weight was considerably diminished. Bond was the final witness called by the prosecution and the next day the defence case would begin and Mark would give evidence. Our defence team had a meeting with Mark in the cells after the prosecution case had closed and we were pleased with the way in which Adrian Fulford QC had really destroyed the credibility of Beech but how would Mark come over, particularly in cross-examination from James Hunt QC?

On Tuesday 26 July, Mark was sworn in and his examination-in-chief began. He recounted where he was and what he was doing on the days leading up to the murder and immediately thereafter. He denied that any discussion ever took place between himself and Beech relating to the murder of his wife and described the allegations made by Beech as "crazy" and told the court he was "amazed" when he read Beech's statements incriminating him and he only knew of Beech's involvement in the murder through the police.

When James Hunt QC stood to begin his cross-examination, we all knew that this could be the most important exchange that would take place. Mark admitted he had bribed people who were supplying books to him so that he could sell the books on rather than having them pulped but denied he was a fraudster. It was also suggested that Mark had a large cash sum at Stable House to pay Beech but Mark replied, "None of it was ever going to David Beech. I can say that one hundred percent." Mark was then asked why Beech would write letters implicating him in the murder. Mark replied, "There is no logic to it. I cannot give any reason. It is something I have been trying to answer myself." Beech's claim that he could never say "no" to Mark was put to him. Mark replied, "I never would believe I have that hold over anyone." At the end of his cross-examination, James Hunt QC put it to Mark that he was cheating in business, cheating on his wife and thought he could get away with anything. Mark strongly denied this assertion and said, "Sarah was the central platform of my life. She made me as strong as I am. My existence without her will be very difficult to continue. The very last person I would want to destroy is Sarah."

It was then for James Hunt QC to sum up the case for the jury. He asserted that the key to the guilt of Mark Williams was the paper and ink of the letters penned by his killer friend David Beech. He repeated his words from his opening speech, "This is not a case of whodunit. We know who did it, but who got him to do it? Was it Mark Williams? Or was it an idea which came quite independently from David Beech? We say to you, quite starkly, that it was Mark Williams' hand behind it." Mr Hunt told the jury there were three important issues they must consider – that the murder was planned, that the plan set out the motive and that the other evidence supported the motive. He said it was undisputed that the murder was pre-planned, because the letters written by David Beech – which claimed Mark Williams asked Beech to kill his wife and which police found in a search of Beech's home – were posted by recorded delivery before the murder took place. And Mr Hunt told the jury that if they had any pangs of doubt about Williams' guilt, they should turn to the letters and ask themselves; why did Beech write them? Mr Hunt put it to the jury, "Why blame in a letter to be read only when he himself is dead? If Mark Williams is telling the truth, it has got to mean this. This was a plan to blame Mark Williams, falsely in a letter, when he is admitting his part, but he is dead. It would therefore be a plan to destroy himself and take Mark Williams down with him for no reason. That has got to be his case has it not? A plan to not only do it but to destroy him and Williams. It is a ludicrous suggestion." Mr Hunt said that apart from the motive claimed by Beech – that Williams ordered him to kill his wife – the evidence heard in court did not support any other motive for the murder. He asked the jury to look at whether Beech's demeanour in the dock had the hallmarks of someone acting or someone who was frightened of the man he was accusing. He added "Remember; that man (Beech) could not speak and had to be cajoled into continuing and took a sip of water because his mouth was so dry. Was he acting that? He could hardly bring himself to say a lot of it." Mr Hunt said Beech would have had to hate Williams to devise a plan to implicate his best friend, "The man who had given him everything." He went on to describe Williams' character – dubbing him "assertive", "strong", "persuasive", "persistent", "predatory" and "a conman." "We say that he tried to con you", added Mr Hunt to the jury. He said that Williams conceded to the police in interview that he was a conman – convincing people he was buying books for pulp, but instead selling them on at a profit. "The fact that he bribes and corrupts does not make him a murderer, but it makes him a liar and difficult to believe," added Mr Hunt. "We know he is accustomed to paying people to do his will. He is accustomed to paying people to commit crimes. He is running a web of deceit, a web into which Beech, the ideal candidate, is recruited." Describing Beech to the jury, Mr Hunt said: "He is a murderer. He is worse than that, on his own account he is an ordered murderer, he is one who was paid to do it. He is a man damned for the rest of his life." In summing up, Mr Hunt added that evidence from the other witnesses was consistent with Beech's story.

Adrian Fulford QC then stood up and addressed the jury, saying that the prosecution had failed at every conceivable level to prove Williams was guilty of murder. He said, "The evidence that has been called before you that my client ordered the murder of his own wife is wholly inconceivable. One demonstration of underlying weakness and desperation is that they end up before you in this Court calling someone of the calibre of John Bond when all else had failed." Describing Bond, who met Williams in prison, as a "professional criminal with a history of perjury", he claimed the prosecution had used him to help prop up "the unbelievable David

Beech". Mr Fulford called into question the motive given by the Crown that Williams had wanted rid of his wife because she wanted children and he did not. He said, "Do you murder the person that is putting that suggestion to you? I say to you that is completely over the top." He told the jury to look at the evidence of prosecution witnesses Joe Azzopardi and the mistress, which he said was vital. He continued, "What does the mistress say to you? These are incredibly important words. If you forget everything else, I hope these remain with you. The mistress gave you evidence about what the defendant was saying to her about the state of his relationship with his wife." He said, "They, Sarah Williams and himself were good friends and he did not want to hurt her." He asked the jury to put that into the context of Williams' relationship with the mistress. He added, "When she said to the defendant she did not want it to go further, the defendant did not kick up at all. He did not say, I want to leave my wife, I want us to run away together. That does not sound like a man desperate to leave his wife." Mr Fulford dismissed earlier evidence that Williams said a divorce would be too costly and said the wealthy businessman could easily have afforded it. He added, "That is about as unimpressive an explanation or motive for killing your spouse as you could get." He told the court that to believe Williams was involved you had to set the motive against the risk. He said, "Is there a really strong motive, something compelling, something that would really drive this man to do a terrible thing and also take the risk?" He said the method used did not fit in with the plan David Beech alleged. The Court was told by Mr Fulford, "David Beech said this had to be a fool-proof plan. Was there anything done by Mark Williams to keep this fool-proof, apart from saying to Beech, 'Keep it simple?'" He said that after Beech allegedly told Williams he would not use the paving slab, by leaving Beech to decide what to use, the plan was not fool-proof. Mr Fulford went on to talk about Beech's allegations about being paid to commit the murder. He told the court, "No arrangements were made before or after the death to hand over the £18,000." Mr Fulford painted a picture of Beech as someone with no grasp of common sense, logic or reason. He described Beech as "weird" and said there was something deeply peculiar about him. He told the court, "It means you cannot rely on David Beech to do or to say things for everyday sensible reasons. The usual standards do not apply to David Beech." At the end of his summing up, Mr Fulford asked the question, "Why did David Beech kill my client's wife?" He told the court, "Some psychiatrist one day may hear the truth about this, but that is speculation, that is a story for the future. For now you may believe underneath something personal was going on, something private to David Beech, something illogical. You will never know what his true motive was. What is unbelievable is that man (Williams) was behind it, that he was the author, that person that put in place the fool-proof plan. We submit that this prosecution has utterly failed." He then sat down.

His Honour Justice Morland then summed up the case for the jury. He warned the jury to treat David Beech's evidence with "extreme caution" and told them if they were convinced his story was truthful they should convict. He added, "When interviewed by the police he lied time and time again and the case against Williams primarily rests on the evidence of Beech. The Judge also said the evidence of John Bond, a convict who claimed Williams confessed the murder to him whilst they were inmates in Nottingham Prison must be treated similarly. He added, "Williams' admittance to an affair, visiting prostitutes, as well as his shady business dealings should not be held against him." At 1.00pm on Thursday 27 July, the jury were discharged by the Judge to consider their verdict.

On the morning of Friday 28 July the front entrance of Nottingham Crown Court was a mass of local and national journalists and radio and television interviewers and their crews. The jury had not immediately come to a decision. After a couple of hours of waiting, the tension was becoming unbearable and suddenly the clerk to the court told us that the jury had reached a verdict. The jury had been deliberating for nine and a half hours. All the relevant parties took their places and Mark was seated in the dock. The Judge came in and asked the foreman of the four men, eight women jury if they had reached a decision. He confirmed they had and he was asked whether the decision was unanimous and the foreman confirmed it was. Mark was standing and holding on to the rail at the front of the dock. The verdict he was about to hear, after an 11 day trial, would determine whether he was to receive a life sentence for murder or whether he would walk out of the Court a free man. The Court was hushed. His Honour Justice Morland asked for the verdict. "Not guilty", replied the foreman. Mark swayed and grasped the rail and then slumped back into his seat. There were cheers from Mark's supporter in the public gallery. The Judge told Mark he was free to go and adjourned the Court for an hour to deal with the sentencing of David Beech.

The defence team went down to the cells where Mark was collecting his personal belongings and of course everybody was jubilant. Understandably, Mark did not want to talk to the press and my solicitor colleague, Robert Starr, did a few interviews and gave a few quotes to the media, saying how relieved Mark was. After about an hour, Mark left the court, driven away by his brother, to go back to Stable House and to start to rebuild his life.

The court reconvened and Beech was brought up from the cells to receive his sentence. He was represented by Guy Boney QC, who said in mitigation it would be very grave for Beech if the Judge took the view that his conspiracy story implicating Williams was concocted merely to "take the heat off himself." The Judge interjected, "I say in open court that this is not my view." Mr Boney dismissed suggestions, made during cross-examination in Williams' case that Beech had killed Mrs Williams because he was having an affair with her and she had threatened to tell her husband. He said, "We would submit the more prosaic explanation that when Mark Williams started to plan his wife's death, he thought that fortune had played into his hands." Beech, a "weak, unscrupulous but personable" individual, had been the ideal candidate to commit the crime, Mr Boney suggested. Beech's decision to turn Queen's evidence indicated his remorse. The result of this decision was that he had received threats to his life and he faced a long period in solitary confinement for his own protection. The Judge, in delivering sentence, told Beech, "You were the actual cold-blooded murderer of a woman who, seconds before you attacked her, was treating you as a friend and with whom you falsely pretended to be friendly. It is, however, to your credit that you have pleaded guilty and, at risk to your own life, have given evidence for the Crown which in my view was probably essentially truthful but I am satisfied that, whatever other reasons there may have been for committing the terrible crime that you did, your primary motive was financial reward."

Beech was given a life sentence but the highly unusual assessment by the Judge gave the media a field day. The next day all the national newspapers ran similar headlines along the lines of, "Body in the pool husband is cleared." The Sun newspaper ran with the story on the front page with a headline: "Cleared but Judge hints jury was wrong."

Detective Chief Superintendent Chris Cook, in charge of the murder investigation for Lincolnshire Police said, "We must abide by the jury's decision but we are not looking for anyone else in connection with this case. The police prosecution did rely heavily on the evidence of Mr Beech." He also indicated that Mark's business dealings would be investigated. The Daily Express who obtained a quotation from an Inland Revenue spokesperson said, "We do not comment on individual cases but it is a general policy to look at all sources of information regarding tax evasion, including the court's." The Guardian concluded that although Mark left the court a free man, his reputation was in shreds as he was revealed as a fraudster, unfaithful and a tax fiddler. The Sun added to their coverage with an interview with Barbara Nutcher-Palmer, with her giving details of her love-making sessions with Beech and an interview with the mistress declaring about Mark that she, "Never wanted to see him for the rest of her life."

Mark was originally arrested in November and until the time he was acquitted at the end of July the following year, this case totally absorbed my professional life. Initially, with Court appearances and then travelling from Peterborough to Nottingham Prison at least twice per week and going through voluminous bundles of documents and statements provided by the CPS and the police.

Then, with the verdict on 28 July, as suddenly as the case had begun it had ended. Other than tidying up a few loose ends and dealing with the media, all the intense work and pressure created by such a serious high profile case suddenly came to an end. I must admit it took a few weeks to get back to reality and the more mundane world of dealing with petty criminals and divorces.

We started to receive proposals from national newspapers and magazines for Mark to sell his story for substantial five figure sums. Back at Stable House, Mark really did want to get on with his life and put the whole ordeal behind him. Despite the substantial sums he was offered to sell his story he declined all of them, choosing instead to give interviews to The Peterborough Evening Telegraph and the Middlemarch Mercury and to do an interview on the local commercial radio station. The Sunday Mirror ran a story giving details of a £150,000 windfall Mark would receive as a result of a pay-out on a life policy on Sarah's death, taken out as part of the mortgage on Stable House. They also revealed that Sarah's family were unhappy with the jury's verdict and had taken advice about a possible OJ Simpson style civil action case against Williams for her unlawful death.

The story started to die down until The Daily Mail did a story on 23 October showing a photograph of Mark and his mistress holding hands, strolling along a beach on holiday in Israel. The Daily Star ran a story in November asserting that Mark had gained a £500,000 inheritance on Sarah's death and finally The Observer did a story in November giving details of the case and how Sarah's family wanted Mark's business dealings investigated by the police. Mark continued living at Stable House for a while but sold it to a neighbour a year after the trial ended and moved away from the immediate area. He has since re-established himself as a successful businessman.

Once everything had settled down I did ask Mark to reflect on the devastating events that arose on that night in October at Stable House. He felt that his personality, being cool and assured and confident worked for him when he was being interviewed in the police station and when giving evidence at the Crown Court Trial but he very much felt it was used against him by the police and the media when it suited them to describe him as "cold, unemotional and calculating." The general public generally do not realise how the police, court and prison systems work against an accused person. When Mark was originally arrested and charged he was remanded into prison and placed in solitary confinement for about seven days "for his own safety." As far as I was aware, there was absolutely no evidence to suggest that Mark was suicidal but just try to picture the circumstances – he was dealing with the death in violent circumstances of his wife, he was charged with her murder, he faced financial and emotional ruin and if convicted of the charges, life in prison. However, cool, cold, calculating, or whatever other adjectives were used to describe him he was clearly under huge pressure and stress. Once he was in a more regular routine in HM Prison Nottingham, he had the forces and power of the state working against him, trying to establish his guilt; the police, the prison authorities and the courts. Mark understood that at one time there had been seventy-two police officers of various ranks working on the case. Although there are plenty of other inmates in prison it is still a lonely, threatening and dangerous place. Clearly, the police in this case had "agents" working on their behalf, whether as fellow inmates or prison officers trying to get further evidence from Mark to strengthen the prosecution case. As a result, Mark could not get close to or trust anyone, thus further adding to his isolation. His contact with the outside world was also limited with only three two hour visitor orders per month plus of course legal visits from myself. I have never checked the statistics but I believe that it is exceptional for a person to be charged with murder in domestic circumstances, to have a lengthy trial and to be acquitted by a unanimous jury of all charges.

Mark did think about taking action against the police and was initially advised against it to enable him to get back to normality much quicker rather than having a civil case against the police running for years at considerable cost and uncertain outcome. He tells me now that he wishes he had pursued that action and he would have been successful. We will never know!

My first school photograph taken when I was five years old. Clearly, I was destined from a young age to a career sitting behind a desk!

Here is my mother Maisie and myself at the front of my childhood home, The Grange, Yaxley. This was a fantastic house to grow up in and I have many fond memories of the house and garden. Unfortunately, the house suffered subsidence and was demolished in the early 1980's.

*I am not sure who thought up the name of this team but here we are, Yaxley Giantkillers –
1966. As was the fashion of the day, nearly all of the team had a nickname. Back Row –
Dubber, Bob, Whack, Dai, Harry, Stanny. Front Row – Dodge (me) Blossom, Bucket,
Derek, Barry. Mascot – Peter, Stanny's younger brother.*

*By 1976, with four of the Yaxley Giantkillers team, Yaxley were the best team in the
Premiership. Unfortunately, the Peterborough and District Premiership. I am in the back
row, second right.*

Here I am in my friend Ishaq's house in the Punjab District of Pakistan with Gazanfer on the left giving me instructions on how to use an AK47. Ishaq on the right seems to have lost interest.

Myself in the middle with Ishaq and the dancing girls in a house in Rawalpindi, Pakistan

Darren Bradshaw, a professional footballer with Peterborough United and myself leaving Peterborough Magistrates Court. Darren had been charged with assault. Darren first gave me the idea to become an Agent representing professional footballers (Photograph courtesy of the Peterborough Evening Telegraph)

In 2000-2001 whilst I was Vice Chairman of Peterborough United, I became involved in a very controversial and acrimonious dispute with the team Manager, Barry Fry, over the terms of his contract. The League Managers Association became involved and the local paper ran with the story on the front and back pages for some time. (Photographs courtesy of the Peterborough Evening Telegraph).

During my involvement with Peterborough United, I had the opportunity to meet some of the great characters involved in professional football. Pictured here are former Manchester United Manager, Tommy Docherty sitting at the desk and behind, left to right, former Liverpool and England legend Phil Neal, Barry Fry, Chris Turner and myself. (Photograph courtesy of the Peterborough Evening Telegraph).

The ultimate sporting legend, George Best and I pictured at a dinner at Peterborough United around 2000. The question I always ask people when I show them this photograph is "Which of these two men allegedly slept with three Miss World's?" Everybody gets it right.

The police and prison authorities received a tip off that there was a plan to "spring" Mark Williams from Nottingham Crown Court when he arrived for the start of his trial for murder. Here, pictured outside the Court building are the armed police officers ready to deal with any problems. (Photograph courtesy of Stephen Daniels)

It is forbidden by law to take photographs inside a Court whilst it is in session. As a result, some very talented artists are commissioned by television companies to sketch the proceedings. This particular sketch was shown on national television during the Mark Williams murder trial and I subsequently purchased the sketch and copyright from the artist. The sketch shows the scene inside the courtroom at Nottingham Crown Court in 2001 with Mark Williams being questioned by Adrian Fulford QC, with the Judge, His Honour Justice Morland in the background.

My good friend, Lee Power, and myself pictured in the boardroom at Luton Town Football Club, Kenilworth Road, Luton after we had been appointed Chairman and Vice Chairman. Lee does not look his usual chirpy, cheerful self. (Photograph courtesy of the Peterborough Evening Telegraph).

This photograph was taken outside the Luton Town Ground at Kenilworth Road whilst Lee and I were in the Boardroom. The anger and hostility of the crowd made it very easy to decline our appointments and any further involvement with the club. (Photograph courtesy of the Peterborough Evening Telegraph).

Peter Boizot, the founder of the Pizza Express chain of restaurants and later owner and Chairman of Peterborough United, presenting myself and my wife Cherry with the Investors in People award in 2000

Staff at Terrells Solicitors pictured outside our office celebrating our decision to give an extra day annual leave on the 23 April each year for St. George's Day. (Photograph courtesy of the Peterborough Evening Telegraph).

Staff members and I celebrating after Terrells Solicitors received a business award in 2009

My father Pat, my son Edward and myself pictured on the pitch at Peterborough United in around 2000

My son Edward, daughter Lucy, wife Cherry and I pictured at a family celebration in the Haycock Hotel, Wansford

7. Up The Posh!

Peterborough United Football Club is known as "The Posh". My father, Frank Terrell, had been a director of The Posh from the early 1950s when they were a Midland League team until their election to the Football League in 1960 to replace Gateshead until about 1967 when he resigned after a dispute with the then manager, Gordon Clark. As a result, I have always loved football but only supported one team – "The Posh." I remember going to my first game, fascinated by the bright colours the teams wore and the chanting and shouting of the fans and the wonderful smell of pipe tobacco emanating from the old fenland farmers who were season ticket holders in the main stand and who would be puffing away on their pipes on a Saturday afternoon once they had been to the cattle market in the morning. The highlight of this period was in January 1965 when The Posh beat mighty Arsenal in the third round of the FA Cup in front of a crowd of over thirty thousand. Eventually, they lost 5-1 to Chelsea at Stamford Bridge in front of over sixty thousand people and we were considerably hampered by the captain, Vic Crowe, being injured and being a passenger for most of the game, in the days before substitutes were allowed. However, the highlights were few and far between and most of the time involved battling away in the old third and fourth divisions against the likes of Colchester, Stockport and the local derby against the Cobblers; Northampton Town.

Over the years, whatever my commitments and wherever I was living, I would get to as many games as possible. Much later, I remember my son Edward, about ten years old at that time, and myself driving up to watch Peterborough play at Spotland against Rochdale on a cold February Saturday afternoon. Just as we passed Rochdale cemetery, by a pub called unbelievably "The Cemetery", I said to my son, "Isn't it a shame that granddad supported The Posh and not Manchester United or Arsenal, so it means that me, and now you, have to support The Posh." He did not seem particularly impressed one way or the other and just grunted and continued playing on his Game Boy. Nick Hornby, in his book "Fever Pitch" discussed this dilemma that most proper football supporters have for their local team rather than the glory supporters of Manchester United, Arsenal and Chelsea, with no real affinity for the club, except they like a team that usually wins. Mind you, Nick Hornby was an Arsenal supporter. Perhaps a better example is TV presenter Adrian Chiles with his love of West Bromwich Albion. Anyway, there it is; once a Posh supporter always a Posh supporter. Against this background, it was a great treat for me when Posh legend Chris Turner came to see me in about 1990 with a fairly mundane conveyancing transaction. Chris had played the one time we played Manchester United at Old Trafford. We only lost 3-1. He was also captain of the team when they were promoted from the old Division Four to Division Three when another Posh legend, Noel Cantwell, was manager. Forget the conveyancing transaction; this gave me the opportunity to quiz Chris about his career and the people in the game. It was fantastic and yes, I was like a real anorak. Chris had gone into management when his playing career ended and had built up a very successful side with John Beck as his assistant at Cambridge United. There had, as usual in football, been some disagreement between Chris and the Cambridge United board of directors and he had been out of work for a few months and was just driving a van for a builder mate of his whilst he was in between jobs. As I later found out, Chris Turner could be the nicest man you could ever meet or the most difficult man you could ever meet, depending on his mood. However, he did confide in me that the chairman of The Posh, an Oxfordshire businessman named John Devaney, had become disillusioned by the lack of success of Mark Lawrenson and his successor Dave Booth. He also confided that he thought he would be getting the manager's job at Peterborough

United in the next few weeks and if he did get the job he would make sure that he referred to me any of the players who needed legal help or advice. That gesture was extremely kind of him and something I will never forget. True to his word, Chris was duly appointed as manager in 1991. At the time, Posh were in the old Division Four but the leagues were being restructured and Posh were quite well placed for the last automatic promotion spot. Promotion or not, all came down to the last game of the season, playing Chesterfield at their old Saltergate ground. Posh only needed a draw but were, at half-time in front of a huge following from Peterborough, 2-0 down. Whatever Chris said at half-time, the team rallied and Dave Robinson and George Berry scored in the second half to secure a 2-2 draw and promotion. The Posh fans went delirious and the reputation of Chris Turner was further enhanced.

Now, it may sound clichéd and stereotypical of certain sections of the population, but in my fairly extensive experience, professional footballers are very good at committing motoring offences, including drink driving, and getting involved in fracas in and outside pubs and night clubs. The players at Posh were no exception and I had a steady stream of players appearing before the local courts to sort out these problems, all referred to me by Chris Turner. The next season, 1991/1992, the Chris Turner formula was again successful. Liverpool were beaten in what was then called the Coca Cola Cup at London Road and Posh reached the Division Two (old Division Three) play-off final after a hard fought play-off semi-final against Huddersfield. The play-off final was at Wembley on a beautiful hot day at the end of May 1992. The Posh won 2-1 with a second goal in the dying minutes from striker Ken Charley. The whole city of Peterborough celebrated and the following day there was a civic reception at the Town Hall and the usual open-top bus tour by the players and officials with thousands lining the streets. The reputation of Chris Turner as manager and bringer of success was still further enhanced. Season 1992/1993 was to be the first season ever that Posh had played in the second tier of English football, now called the Championship, against the likes of Derby County, Newcastle United, West Ham, Sunderland and Wolverhampton Wanderers, instead of the usual diet of Colchester, Stockport etc. John Devaney was still the owner of the club but I heard via Chris Turner that he wanted to sell due to ill health and to concentrate on his other business interests. Chris told me he was getting a consortium together with an old friend of his, a wealthy local businessman named Alf Hand, and another local businessman called Sean Reilly. Chris told me if they did go ahead he would give me a call and I could do the necessary legal work involved in the takeover. This was an exciting opportunity and although involving fairly complex company and commercial issues, was well within my capability. For all football supporters of their local club, there is something intriguing and fascinating about the stadium, the behind-the-scenes, the players, everything about it. To have the opportunity to get involved in all these things is very exciting. In addition, the local media, in our case, The Peterborough Evening Telegraph, and the local radio and television stations rely heavily on events happening at the local football team. As I was to discover later, this can be a double-edged sword.

On a Thursday lunchtime at the beginning of December 1992, the call came through from Chris. He said, "We are in a meeting in the boardroom at London Road with John Devaney and his representatives, can you get straight down here?" I left my office immediately and got to go through the official entrance at the ground and into the boardroom where I had not been for about twenty years, since the days when my father was a director. Everything seemed much smaller than I could remember but it had hardly changed. I was introduced to all the parties and my work really began. Clients are not really bothered about any legal problems, time limitations or anything else legal. They just want the job doing as quickly, always as quickly, as possible at a minimal cost. This job was no exception and we got the job done ready for the press conference on Friday 19 December 1992. I was on the panel for the press conference. Chris Turner had been appointed chairman with his assistant manager/coach Lil Fuccillo being appointed team manager. Chris read out a statement, which I had drafted: "Due to the speculation of and uncertainty surrounding the future of Peterborough United going back over several months, Chris Turner, Alf Hand, and Sean Reilly have this afternoon purchased the football club. In doing so, we have had to beg, steal and borrow a substantial sum of money to put the club back where it belongs – in the hands of the Peterborough people." We were all on a real high, it was mid-December but Christmas had come a few days early. I was now really progressing in the world of professional football and moving from representing players to being the legal advisor to my home team professional football club. However, as I was to learn later, the job could provide the rollercoaster of tremendous stress, heartache and negative publicity as well as the joy and excitement of success. I think all professional football clubs in England in all divisions both then in the early nineties and now really struggle to balance income from gate receipts, sponsorship, advertising, and transfer fees against expenditure, mainly on players' wages. Posh did have an advantage in that they had developed offices at the ground which they let out to the Probation Service at an excellent rent and had other commercial units rented out to hairdressers, bookmakers etc and a night club which was very successful in catering for the Peterborough singles market, christened by Chris Turner as the "grab-a-granny-night." From December 1992, Chris Turner and Alf Hand worked extremely hard in keeping costs down and maximising income, including income from transfers. For the financial year ended May 1993, a profit of £880,000 was made and £654,000 for May 1994. By May 1995 there was a loss of £210,000 and in May 1996 over £600,000. It was the usual equation of keeping the good players and having success on the field or selling and struggling on the field. All the fans were interested in, quite rightly, was success on the field at any cost. In 1994, I was appointed a director of the club. I was carrying out a lot of legal work for the club at the time in relation to various litigation matters and leases of properties. With hindsight I think my appointment was a clever ploy by Chris Turner and Alf Hand to keep their legal fees down rather than anything else, but it did give me the authority and privilege to have the best tickets for games home and away and to meet some of the very interesting characters involved with professional football clubs. Notwithstanding the ongoing financial constraints, the atmosphere and commitment of everyone involved at the club was excellent. There was a real spirit engendered by Chris and Alf that we were all in it together from the board of directors to the players, managers, the backroom staff and the programme sellers. Everybody wanted to help and make the club better and there was no sniping and backbiting.

About a week before the end of the 1995/1996 season, I got a call from Chris Turner's wife, Lynne. Chris had been rushed into hospital the previous day as an emergency. He had collapsed and was experiencing severe stomach pain. He had been diagnosed with peritonitis. He had undergone lengthy surgery which had involved removing part of his stomach and intestines. He was going to be in hospital for a few days recovering from the surgery and would then have to convalesce at home. I went to see Chris at the Fitzwilliam Hospital and clearly he had undergone very serious surgery which had left him quite weak. He told me that he had been advised that continued stress had caused the condition to develop and there was no way he could continue to be involved with the day-to-day stress of running the football club as he had previously been. He had to slow down or he would be dead, his medical team had told him. Although Chris had been running the club with Alf Hand, Alf could not take on the running of the club himself and a solution would have to be found. In the short time since his surgery, Chris had been thinking about options but the only real option was a change in ownership of the football club. Chris was discharged from hospital to his home and a couple of days later he called me to say he had set up a meeting with Barry Fry at his house to discuss a business proposition and could I be there? Chris had always been friendly with Barry. Barry had been manager at Barnet, Southend United and Birmingham City. Chris had done some coaching for Barry at Barnet and Chris always told the story that they went on to the training ground and the players had been out earlier doing some warm-ups. When they came into view, Chris said it was like the cavalry coming and he had never coached so many players in one session. Barry had a reputation for having large playing squads and buying and selling players. Chris had been involved in selling central defender Gary Breen and Peterborough United goalkeeper Ian Bennet to Barry Fry's Birmingham City for substantial fees. Barry was extremely popular with the media for his cavalier attitude and clever comments. He was, and is, a genuinely humorous man and very sociable but, as we later found out, he does have a darker side. Barry had just had his contract at Birmingham City terminated by the Gold brothers and David Sullivan. He was looking for a new challenge. Many people in football, myself included, thought Barry had been harshly treated by Birmingham City. He was one of the most exciting managers around outside the Premier League, with an obvious talent for publicity and a wheeler/dealer in buying and selling players for a profit.

Peterborough United was quite unusual as a football club in that it had the traditional football income of gate receipts, perimeter advertising, match and shirt sponsorship, TV money and transfer fee income (if any) but also income generated from letting surplus space at the stadium to the Cambridgeshire Probation Service, a hairdressing salon, a betting office and a pub and a nightclub. It had always been the medium to long-term plan to form a second limited company and transfer all the non-football income and assets to that company and leave all the football income, assets and liabilities in the old football company. The plan made commercial sense but would need some fairly complex legal and accounting work to put it into effect. The day of the meeting with Barry Fry arrived and Chris, Barry, Alf Hand and myself all attended at Chris and Lynne's house in Ramsey Forty Foot, a village about ten miles from Peterborough, for the meeting which, as we were to discover later, would change the whole future of Peterborough United Football Club. Chris was still recovering from his surgery and was confined to bed. Therefore, his wife Lynne had to organise the bedroom and furniture to make sure we all had a seat. Chris and Alf had obviously had a discussion before the meeting and they had decided that their original long-term plan of splitting the club into two limited companies and dividing the football and non-football income could be implemented straightaway. The existing Peterborough United Football Club Ltd would retain ownership of the stadium and all non-football income. This company would continue to be owned in the majority by Chris and Alf and they would receive the net income generated by the non-football activities. A new company would then be formed, called Peterborough United F.C. (1996) Ltd, and all the football income, including the players' registrations and gate receipts etc would be owned by this company. Barry would get one hundred percent of the shares of this company for nothing and he could finance and run the company how he chose and get in whoever he wished as investors or partners. It was his company and he could do as he wanted. We had a discussion and the principles of the proposed arrangement suited both camps. Chris and Alf were happy with the income generated by non-football activities without the hassle, aggravation and stress of running a football club and Barry could have what he had always dreamed of; ownership of a football club and for nothing. They were very happy and as usual could not wait to get on with it. However, I did caution them all that there were very complex legal, financial and accounting procedures to be followed and approvals to be gained from slow moving bureaucratic organisations such as the Inland Revenue, HM Customs & Excise, The Football League, The Football Association and the club's bankers, Barclays Bank. To the parties, these formalities were not important - they were football people and just wanted to get on with the publicity, signing players and football aspects generally and worry about the other matters later. Unfortunately the "later" arrived sooner than anticipated. As part of the new set up, Chris and Alf were to remain as directors but neither wanted to be chairman. Barry did not want to be chairman as he was going to be a "hands-on" football manager. So, the only person left to do the job by default was me. In June 1996, I was appointed as chairman of Peterborough United Football Club. With wonderful hindsight, the deal was far too hastily put together and very poorly thought through. Barry was interested in football and he had very little knowledge or experience on how to run the financial side of a football club. Recently, he had been used to working with money provided by multi-millionaires and had no financial involvement himself. He had no idea how to properly plan, budget and finance a football club with a multi-million pound turnover. Even more unbelievable was that he took little or no financial advice prior to launching into the venture. Barry was very anxious to deal with the matters that interested him. One of the first things he did was to give himself a very lucrative contract, with an excellent basic salary and bonuses. Barry later claimed that I had prepared his contract. This was totally incorrect. I had prepared and provided the wording of the contract document but with the figures left blank. Barry had decided the figures himself and put them in the contract. There had never been a board meeting to discuss his salary. He decided to pay himself what he thought he was worth. All of us would love that opportunity. In addition, it was always understood by the other board members that the fairly substantial additional income Barry received from his other media activities would be paid to the club and retained by the club. This did not happen.

A press conference was called and the plan was announced. Whatever limitations Barry had with his knowledge of finances, he was a master of publicity and the venture was very well received by supporters with the usual, "I'll take you out of this league." Season ticket sales reached levels not seen for many seasons. The problem with season ticket sales is that it is immediate income but it is advance payment on sales which are a large part of the income for the next twelve months. Barry started signing players and paid a large transfer fee to sign Martin O'Connor and Scott Houghton from Walsall. The separation of the club into two and, more importantly, the separation of the bank accounts had not been implemented. Matters were taking longer than even I had anticipated. As the season started, despite spending transfer fees and signing plenty of new players, the performance on the field was poor. By October/November 1996, Barry had started looking in more detail at the finances of the club and had finally brought in some financial advice and discovered that the club could not continue as it was. Barry then started putting stories out in the local media that he was not in charge, which was true, but he failed to mention that it had been agreed that there would be the structure previously mentioned. Barry also told the local paper that the players' form had been affected by the financial problems as the team plunged towards the bottom of Division Two (now Division One). Whatever the rights and wrongs of the situation, it was amazing that the disaster had happened so quickly. There was no doubt that the club needed a financial saviour as quickly as possible but where would one be found? Multi-millionaires with spare cash for a club like Posh were not common. The previous united front under the ownership of Chris and Alf had changed and the atmosphere was hostile and back-biting and people involved at the club were falling out and talking behind backs as never before.

I had not heard of Keith Cheesman before I met him at The Ramada Hotel in Peterborough in December 1996. Barry Fry had introduced him to the club. He was described as an Essex businessman and Barry knew him from his days as manager of Dunstable when Cheesman owned that club. Cheesman was a fat, balding man in his mid-forties, accompanied by a very glamorous younger woman, dripping with gold jewellery. My wife Cherry and I met him in the bar at the hotel and he was there to impress and make it clear he was a man of substantial wealth. He was an engaging man, full of stories about himself and extremely generous. He insisted all drinks were shorts and ordered them as what he called "a friendly", which meant "a double". He was full of his life stories. Apparently, he was interested in purchasing a football club within a reasonable distance of London. He could then promote live music concerts. That is what he did and, according to him, he had amazing contacts. He would drop sentences into the conversation like, "Gloria's got a bad back." "Gloria? Who is Gloria?" I would ask. He would say, "Gloria Estefan. I have been on the phone to her in Florida this morning" or, "Frank's not been well." "Frank?" "Frank Sinatra." I did not know whether to believe him or not and I said, cynically, "I bet you'll say you know the Pope next." Funnily enough, he said, "I had an audience with the Pope last year in the Vatican." At the same time, he was meeting with Barry Fry, Chris Turner, Alf Hand and other important figures at the club trying to win them over. I must admit he was really good company, very friendly and very generous. I was just unsure as to whether you could believe a word he said. On the last occasion we had a drink together, he said to the manager of the hotel, "There you go, you won the bet. You said I would get my bar bill up to £1,000 and I did not think I would do it." The manager smiled as Cheesman gave him a £50.00 note. As quickly as he had appeared and offered to put £1 million into the club, Cheesman disappeared. Then slowly the truth about him began to emerge. Somebody, somehow, came across a DVD of a BBC documentary called "The Biggest Robbery In The World" which told the story of how Bank of England bearer bonds, worth £392 million, had been stolen in London at knife point. The robbers tried to launder them through the IRA in Northern Ireland and the mafia in Florida and eventually Keith Cheesman was arrested at his luxury Barbican apartment in London. He jumped bail and went to Tenerife but he was recaptured and extradited to the USA to stand trial. A total of twenty five people were arrested. One of Cheesman's co-conspirators, Mark Osborne, was found in the boot of a car in Houston, Texas, shot twice in the back of the head. In 1993, Cheesman was convicted and sentenced to six and a half years in prison. Therefore, when we had our meetings with him he could not have been long out of prison. Barry must have known his history because it then transpired that when he had been the owner of Dunstable Football Club and Barry the manager, they had unbelievably signed George Best and Jeff Astle. The glory was very short lived however and the club shut down, overwhelmed by debts. In 1977, Cheesman was convicted of defrauding a US finance company and sentenced to six years imprisonment. I have to admit, Cheesman was a real character and very entertaining to be around but he was a professional criminal. I remember watching a crime documentary after all this blew over and Cheesman was there conspiring with a very attractive bank worker to provide him with funds. I believe he was convicted and sentenced to a bit more time in prison. A few weeks later, I received a telephone call from Cambridgeshire Police asking if I knew Cheesman's whereabouts as he had vacated the hotel after a long stay but had omitted to pay his bill, running into several thousand pounds! We heard nothing further from Cheesman and I wonder where he is now? By January 1997 the pressure to find a buyer was becoming intense and then along came the perfect candidate; Mr Peter Boizot. Peter Boizot was born and bred in Peterborough. He attended the Cathedral School, the Kings School and St Catharine's College, Cambridge before he went off to Europe to seek his fortune. He came back to London in 1965 with an idea he got from his time in Italy to open a pizza restaurant. He spoke with his bank manager, accountant, solicitor and they all said he was mad. A dough base, with mushrooms, cheese and tomato would never work - it was ridiculous. Peter was undaunted and despite the objections of those around him, he opened his first pizza restaurant and then others and eventually floated the business known as Pizza Express and made a fortune. After years away, he had returned to Peterborough and set up various business ventures in the city, including The Great Northern

Hotel, Gastons Restaurant and The Broadway Theatre. Alf Hand had also been a pupil at The King's School and Peter and Alf knew each other from years gone by. Peter wanted to do the deal and on 23 January 1997, at a press conference at the ground, he was unveiled as the new owner and saviour of the club. Peter's passion was jazz music and a jazz band provided the music at the event. The deal left Barry as manager with a substantial contract for a manager of a club near the bottom of the league, Chris Turner as Football Co-ordinator, Alf Hand as a director, and I stepped down from Chairman to Vice-Chairman. Peter had his own team of lawyers and I was no longer involved in any legal work for the club. Peter Boizot is an extremely nice, generous man but totally eccentric, in a good way, with a taste for the good things in life: food, wine, jazz and theatre. He is a total contrast to Barry Fry who is a brash, loud, no-nonsense football man, but the two opposites attracted and got on extremely well. Barry was quoted at the press conference as saying, "I think Peter Boizot is the best signing this football club will ever make in its history." Barry certainly had the knack of saying the right thing at the right time. Funnily enough, at the press conference, Peter told reporters that his nephew, his solicitor, his stockbroker and basically everyone he spoke to told him not to get involved with Posh because of their debts. He was then asked, "Well, why did you do it then?" He responded that he had received similar warnings prior to his involvement in Pizza Express and he managed to make that business a success so he could do the same with Posh. Posh had debts of £2.5 million and were losing £750,000 per annum. Barry Fry's reign as owner had lasted from May/June 1996 to January 1997. Once Peter Boizot took over at the club, he wanted to introduce his own style and way of doing things. To be fair to Peter, he wanted administratively to run things in a very professional manner and introduced his own solicitors and accountants to deal with the legal and accounting formalities for the club.

On the football side, Peter absolutely loved Barry Fry and would have long conversations and debates with him after each home game in particular. Barry was very clever at making sure more or less whatever he wanted on the playing or coaching side he could have. During Peter's involvement at the club with Barry as manager there were at least twelve assistant managers and coaches to assist Barry, including Phil Neal, Jimmy Quinn, Bobby Gould, Paul Ashworth and Wayne Turner. Their tenure was never long, a bit like being a wife to Henry VIII. They were not beheaded, divorced or died but sacked, resigned or they just walked out. Although chief executives were employed by Peter, they also came and went. Effectively, Barry was running the football club and knew exactly what was going on but the costs were beginning to escalate and Peter Boizot was having to subsidise the running of the club from his own private cash resources. In my view, for the money being spent on the football side compared with other teams in the same league, we were not particularly successful. The highlight was winning the last Division Three (now League Two) play-off final at the old Wembley against Darlington on a Friday evening throughout torrential rain. It gave us all the opportunity to experience the Royal Box and the opposition were owned by ex-safe cracker George Reynolds, who was as eccentric as our Mr Boizot. At the next board meeting after the victory, Barry Fry walked out in a debate over using youth team players in the reserves but spoke with the media and said he had been sacked, which was of course rubbish. A very short time later, Barry returned, saying it was a misunderstanding.

Peter Boizot did not understand football and never pretended that he did, leaving football matters to Barry and his legion of assistants going through the revolving door. He did like detail and for things to look good. I remember we were playing Queens Park Rangers at Loftus Road and the two teams came running out and started warming up. I was sitting next to Peter and he said, "Roger, I am very annoyed, who authorised the new kit? I am not impressed." Peter was looking at the QPR team in their traditional blue and white hoops! I said, "Peter, you are looking at QPR. We are the other end in red, our away kit because of the clash of colours." At another game at Peterborough, he said to me whilst the game was in play, "Roger, did I dream it or did we win 11-0 last week?" I said, "Peter, you definitely dreamt it, as we lost 1-0 at Northampton Town." There are endless other examples but I must stress I have total respect for Peter Boizot, as have all who meet him; he is a lovely, generous, eccentric man. It is unusual for a football club to sponsor events, but under Peter's stewardship, Posh sponsored "The

Art Treasures of England" exhibition at the Royal Academy of Art in Piccadilly, Central London with works by Turner, Canaletto, Gainsborough, Hogarth, Constable, and Hockney. Barry Fry and the whole of the first team squad, the board of directors and various other hangers-on attended to be greeted by Sir Richard Attenborough, Lord Archer (before his disgrace) and Anna Ford. Peter gave a speech and I think Barry Fry did as well. We then all trekked off to Peter's restaurant in Soho called Kettners and all the players went to his pizza restaurant at Hyde Park called "Pizza on the Park." What an evening! On another occasion, Peter sponsored the British Olympic Appeal and asked myself and my wife Cherry, plus Alf and Pat Hand, our co-directors, to attend a fundraising dinner at Kings College, Cambridge. We all travelled together and arrived at the fantastic venue for cocktails before dinner. What Peter had not told us was that we were to be introduced to Princess Anne, who was the patron of the British Olympic Appeal. The five of us were standing there; Peter, Pat, Alf and Cherry and I. Peter introduced himself as chairman of Peterborough United Football Club and us as his co-directors and our wives. Peter then said, "We are known as The Posh, you know." "Really?" asked Princess Anne, and I replied, "It is a long story." She responded, "Well, I am intrigued, do tell it" and then I managed to tell the story of how, in the 1930s, when the club changed the colour of their shirts from green to blue and the team ran out at the London Road ground, a local wag shouted, "They look posh," and the name has stuck ever since and is well known in football circles. Princess Anne, I think, was impressed, thanked me and rapidly moved on. Peter was very keen, quite rightly, on maintaining and promoting "The Posh" name. He instructed his lawyers to register the name as a trademark and they received correspondence from lawyers for Victoria Beckham on the basis that the public would think in some way she had endorsed products she had no knowledge of. Bearing in mind, the Posh have been the Posh since the 1930s, no further action was taken by either party. Another great event I enjoyed, due to the hospitality of Peter Boizot, was a sportsman's dinner with the late legendary George Best and the comedian Stan Boardman. For every man of a certain vintage, George was the ultimate and to meet him and hear him speak and tell all of his wonderful stories was a real treat. I sat on the top table with George, Stan and Barry, and had my obligatory photo taken with him. Ever since that night and since the photograph was developed, I have shown the photo to friends and relatives and any other unfortunate persons who are around and said, "Two people in the photo; one slept with three Miss World's, could have been seven but he did not turn up four times, and the other slept with none. Guess which one?" Everybody gets it right!

Barry Fry is a very sociable, affable chap who has a funny story for every occasion and he is good fun to be with on a social occasion. However, in my view, he was doing a below average job at an above average salary and the club could just not continue with its financial structure the way it was. Peter Boizot was running out of money and the only prospects were a sale or administration. Matters cane to a head at the beginning of 2001/2002 season. It was clear that the club's bankers would not increase the overdraft limit and Peter had run out of any other sources of raising capital to put into a loss making football club. The reality was stark and not what Peter Boizot, Barry Fry, myself and the other board members or the supporters wanted – we had to either find a buyer for the club with substantial funds to cover the debts and running costs on an ongoing basis or the matter would be taken out of everybody's hands by the club going into administration. Other clubs were experiencing similar capital and cash flow problems to those experienced by Posh and Queen's Park Rangers had recently appointed administrators to deal with their financial problems. I did have some preliminary discussions with the accountant approved as liquidator at that club to be aware of the implications should we have no choice but to go down that route. As far as finding a credible purchaser for the club, there were two important issues to take into account. The first issue was the generous contract which Barry Fry had given himself, which was still place. Therefore any potential purchaser would have to keep Barry on as manager, although his track record had been poor, or terminate his contract and pay him substantial compensation. Barry knew that no deal could be done without dealing with this issue and his contract. The second important factor was the eight acres of freehold property on which the London Road stadium was located. The main part of the site on which the stadium was situated was purchased at a nominal price from Peterborough City Council in 1955. The conveyance contained a right of pre-emption in favour of Peterborough City Council in that if it was proposed that the land be sold or transferred, they should have the first option and should have up to six months to decide if they wanted to exercise that option.   In addition, there was a restrictive covenant in the conveyance in favour of Peterborough City Council, which limited the use of this part of the land for sporting purposes. It was understandable that Peterborough City Council, as sellers of this land in 1955, would want to be involved in any future development plan and these restrictions meant that the land could not be dealt with without the agreement and involvement of Peterborough City Council. The remainder of the site at the Moys End part of the stadium, including a large car park had no restrictions and could be dealt with as the then owners of the club deemed appropriate. Therefore, potentially the football club site was worth many millions of pounds, particularly if the club relocated to a new purpose built stadium. The relocation of the club to a new site had been a regular issue over the period of my involvement with the club and various prospective new sites had been suggested.

Myself and fellow directors began to notice that another friend of Barry's called Colin Hill started coming along to games as Barry's boardroom guest. At first nobody really knew very much about Colin Hill. He was usually accompanied by his wife and they kept very much to themselves. Clearly, he was very keen on football and a very good friend of Barry. What was his interest? In November 2001, we played Bedford in the first round of the FA Cup. Without consulting or discussing the matter with the board of directors, Colin Hill was kitted out in a Peterborough United sweatshirt and wearing a tracksuit. He sat next to Barry in the dugout throughout the game. He was described on the team sheet as the club's "financial advisor". His appearance caused much speculation with supporters and the media. It was soon established that he was a very wealthy businessman, property developer and the owner of a Swiss bank. He made a very generous offer of a loan to the club of over £1 million at a friendly interest rate to see the club through its financial difficulties but he had no interest in taking control of the club and he insisted that the proposal was a gesture from a football fanatic, not the first move in a potential takeover. He further confirmed that his interest in the club stemmed from his long friendship with Barry Fry. In my view this was a generous offer but there needed to be a long term solution to the plight of the club, not further borrowing which could never realistically be repaid. The underlying problems at the club needed to be addressed. Too much money had been spent on transfer fees and wages. There was a substantial youth policy which had produced players which had been sold for large fees but the cost of the policy far outweighed the income it generated. It was the cost of developing the majority of players from the youth policy that did not make the grade rather than the handful that were sold for a fee. The pressure to find a buyer for the club intensified and an offer was put to Peter Boizot by a local businessman called Kevin Tatum of £1 million plus a cash injection of £1.5 million. This offer was rejected but Kevin Tatum was still keen to pursue matters further. In December 2001 an advertisement for the sale of a Division Two football club appeared in The Daily Telegraph. We all knew this was an advertisement placed by Peter Boizot. I decided to see how easy or difficult it was to raise finance to buy the club and, bearing in mind the asset value of the land owned by the club, after several meetings with representatives of a public limited company, I got together a package and was able to make Peter Boizot an offer of £1.5 million. As always, Peter Boizot was the perfect gentleman and treated me with respect but he rejected my offer on the basis the club was worth more, which it probably was.

Into the New Year in 2002 and Colin Hill was reconsidering his position and indicating he may be interested in purchasing the club. The uncertainty and indecision surrounding the club was very bad for the morale of everybody connected with the club. The local paper, The Peterborough Evening Telegraph, decided to liven up the debate by inviting supporters to phone in and vote for their preferred bidder/owner of the club. The survey showed thirty-six point nine percent in favour of Colin Hill, me in second place with thirty-six point four, Kevin Tatum third with eighteen point two percent and finally Peter Boizot with eight point five percent.

As we came to the end of the 2001/2002 season, at the last home game against Bury there were angry scenes from some of the Posh supporters calling for, "Boizot and Fry out". This genuinely upset

Peter as he could not believe that after all his investment and genuine commitment, supporters would turn hostile towards him. Stories also started circulating in the local press about the level of wages received by Barry Fry of up to £250,000 per annum, which Barry was quick to dismiss as "rubbish." By the beginning of the 2002/2003 season, Peter had become involved in discussions with a consortium formed by a football agent and a leisure developer calling themselves Peterborough Sporting Club. Peter seemed very keen on dealing with them but they were very slow in moving the purchase forward. By October, the figures for the previous year were released, showing again the club had lost over £1 million for the third time in four years. If matters continued as they were and Peter sold fairly quickly, his losses would be nearly £7.5 million. Nothing seemed to be moving forward with the sale of the club and the losses were running at about £20,000 per week and could not continue. I suggested there should be a reduction in expenses because of the plight of the club. Barry Fry was probably the highest earner at the club and I publicly challenged him to take a pay reduction and reveal how much he actually earned. Although Barry always stated I revealed details of his earnings at the club to the press, which I did not do, The Peterborough Evening Telegraph were tipped off that his earnings had been £233,039 in the last financial year. I do not know where they got their information from and they refused to reveal their sources. Barry was livid and immediately contacted John Barnwell at the League Managers' Association, the managers' union, and accused me of breach of confidence in revealing his earnings to the press. It perhaps did not occur to Barry that I was not the only person who thought that he was paid too much for what he delivered but I was not the person who revealed the details of his contract to The Evening Telegraph and the editor of the newspaper stated in least two articles that I had not revealed the details they had printed. Barry completely ignored this and, in a totally defamatory way, continued with his tirade of criticism of me, seemingly supported by the League Managers' Association. To try and resolve matters, The Evening Telegraph commissioned a phone-in and the fans overwhelmingly voted at sixty-nine percent with the view that he was not worth his salary against thirty-one percent who thought he was. Many supporters felt the same as I did, that Barry Fry was paid too much for what he delivered and at subsequent home matches there was an increasing trend of "Fry Out" chants and banners. In November 2002 we played at Rochdale in the FA Cup and soon went three goals down. A number of Posh supporters left the game at half-time and the ones that remained were hostile to Barry Fry and after the game vented their feelings and anger on local and national radio phone-ins. Bizarrely, for the second half of the game, Colin Hill was standing next to coach Phil Chapple at the front of the dugout shouting and pointing to the players whilst Barry sat in the dugout not taking part. He then did a story in The News of the World saying he was no quitter and that I had disclosed his salary and wanted the club to go into administration so that I could then buy it for next to nothing. This story was, of course, absolutely rubbish! I had already withdrawn from being a prospective purchaser of the club and there was no way Barry would quit the club with his lucrative contract in place. By this time the club was out of all club competitions and second from bottom in the league. With Barry entitled under his contract to ten percent of the value of sales, there was a clear incentive for him to sell players if offers came in. Wigan came in with an offer for Jimmy Bullard, a young mid-fielder who, in fairness to Barry, he had signed on a free transfer. I was very much against the sale of the player as he was an important part of the team. Nevertheless, he was sold and Barry received his ten percent. The sale to Peterborough Sporting Club just dragged on and on and they never met deadlines. As we neared the end of the season all the old financial pressures were still there and there seemed no prospect of a sale.

Colin Hill had, by this time, purchased the club's training ground at Eye and quite properly charged a rent which the club struggled to pay. Prior to the home game against Wigan on 10 March, Colin Hill confronted Philip Sagar, a fellow director and acting chief executive. The discussion became heated and voices were raised and allegedly Colin Hill made a threat to Philip Sagar and his family if the money was not paid. The police were called and statements were taken, although no arrests were made. This confrontation was just one of the many examples of the hostility, uncertainty and unpleasantness surrounding the club at the time. By the end of April and the last game of the season at home to Notts

County, a buyer had finally been found. A football man? A property speculator? A consortium of supporters? No, none other than previous owner and current director Alf Hand. Apparently, the deal had been signed at a local solicitors' office at 2.00pm on the day of the match at a meeting between Alf Hand and his representatives and Peter Boizot and his representatives. For some reason, Barry Fry was also present at the meeting. Apparently, Alf paid £250,000 for Mr Boizot's ninety-nine percent holding and wanted repayment of a sum of £416,000 owed to him by the club and of course he took on liability for the debts. It was reported in the local press that Alf had received financial support from none other than Colin Hill, described as a great friend and supporter of Barry Fry. Alf was quoted as saying, "Peter and I share a common bond. We both love Posh and this city. Neither of us wanted this club's future being driven by property or land consortiums." At the end of the final home game of the season against Notts County, I was having a drink in the bar with two Notts County players who were long-standing friends and clients of mine: Ian Baraclough and Ian Richardson. A message came through to me that I was needed in the boardroom to sign my letter of resignation. I duly attended and signed reluctantly drinking a glass of champagne to celebrate the sale/purchase. It was a sad day for me. There had been a lot of bad times and acrimonious exchanges but, all in all, it had been a fantastic experience to be involved at the highest level in my home town football club. The end of an era for me.

With the help of Alf Hand and Colin Hill, Barry Fry's position as manager was secure but the story did not end there. When the ownership of the club changed hands from Peter Boizot to Alf Hand, there was no mention whatsoever that the club had actually been purchased by a secretive Swiss-registered organisation called the Wetmore Foundation and that Alf Hand was merely a front for that organisation. The spin on the story was that the club had been saved from property developers but before long Barry Fry began to say openly that his property developer/businessman friend, Colin Hill, had bought the club. By October 2003 Wetmore Foundation transferred the ownership of eight acres of prime development land, if sold, or a football stadium if retained, to a company called Peterborough United Holding Ltd for a consideration of £3.5

million. The football side of the business, without ownership of the stadium, was then either given or sold to a company under the majority control of Barry Fry. Ironically, this was exactly what was intended when Barry Fry first became involved with the club. Barry Fry explained, "Colin Hill is a shrewd businessman and he did not want the football club because he said it would always lose money. I am a football person so I took it on." There is no mention of why Alf Hand chose to front the purchase from Peter Boizot. Was it because they were old school friends and knew and trusted each other? If Colin Hill's money and company purchased the club, why did it need to be done in secret? Why did the true nature of the transaction need to be hidden? At the 2003 AGM, Alf Hand commented that the sale of the stadium had not been a good deal for the club. Peterborough City Council still controlled matters and there could not be a change of ownership of the stadium without their consent. Negotiations took place between Colin Hill and his representatives and the legal representatives of Peterborough City Council and Peterborough City Council decided not to exercise their option to purchase the land contained in the 1955 conveyance, being the main stadium site. It is not clear who made this decision but it was not made by elected councillors and must have been under some delegated authority to council officers. Whatever the reason was for the football club to lose its ownership of the freehold of the stadium, there is absolutely no suggestion that anything illegal or improper was done. In 2006 Peterborough United Holding Ltd made a planning application to Peterborough City Council for ninety-six two-bedroom flats and thirty-nine one-bedroom flats plus the development of a new stand at the Moys End section of the ground.

The relationship between Barry Fry, who had been best man at Colin Hill's wedding, broke down and Colin Hill had no involvement with Barry's football side of the business other than being his landlord. Whilst Barry was in control of the football club, the rent was nominal but if a third party become involved the rent would increase to a commercial rent. With the club under Barry's control, the familiar pattern continued with little or no success on the field, expenses too high and regular changes in personnel and plenty of controversy.

In August 2007 Darragh MacAnthony, a Dublin born Marbella based businessman and owner of MRI Overseas Property became the owner of the club, paying a nominal £1 and taking on responsibility for the club's substantial debts and responsibilities. The Sunday Times Rich List estimated his wealth at £150 million in 2007 and £68 million in 2008. A UK subsidiary of MRI, MRI Overseas Property went into voluntary liquidation in April 2010. Barry Fry has remained in his employment but not as team manager. He is presently described as Director of Football and appears to have responsibility for buying and selling players and negotiating their contracts. He also promotes himself as an after-dinner speaker. In January 2010, the company controlled by Colin Hill which controlled the freehold of the Posh ground, sold it to Peterborough City Council for £8.5 million. The City Council continued to lease the facilities to the football club at a commercial rate. Peterborough United Football Club received none of the £8.5 million on the sale of their former asset to Peterborough City Council. In the latest The Sunday Times Rich List, Colin Hill was number three hundred and thirty-seven with an estimated wealth of £200 million accumulated through car repossessions, financing and leasing aircraft, salvage, property and timeshares. Peter Boizot has now withdrawn from the business activities he was involved in whilst he owned the Posh, including the Broadway Theatre in Peterborough, and the Great Northern Hotel which was purchased in 2009 by a company under the control of Colin Hill. Who were the winners and who were the losers in the battle for the control of Posh? I will leave you to decide.

8. An Agent but Nothing Secret

There is no doubt that for a large section of the population, professional football is glamorous and exciting. This allure is added to by the difficulty ordinary supporters have in getting close to the players and getting to know what is going on behind the scenes. All the talk, rumour, and speculation is what many fans and journalists thrive on. From the late eighties and early nineties, there was a real development in professional football with the emergence of agents representing players and those agents becoming as high profile as some their clients, sometimes unfortunately for the wrong reasons. I had got involved in representing professional footballers back in 1990/1991 in connection with legal matters that affected them - fairly mundane stuff such as house conveyancing, allegations of assaults from fights outside night clubs, drink driving and divorce.

In June 1994, Posh player Darren Bradshaw was charged with an assault outside a night club called Muswells in Broadway, Peterborough. We had a two day trial at Peterborough Magistrates' Court and at the end of the trial, despite very strong evidence in Darren's favour from fellow Posh midfielder John McGlashan, Darren was found guilty. Darren was a player that a lot of managers liked and he had a good pedigree. Posh had signed him from Newcastle United but Posh were not looking to renew his contract. At one point, there was a suggestion that the Magistrates' were considering a prison sentence so I arranged for Brendon Batson of the Professional Footballers' Association to come to Court and explain the difficulties for players getting a new club offer after their contract had expired, particularly if they were jailed! The Magistrates took on board what Brendon Batson had said and gave Darren a Community Service Order. Darren and I had a coffee and a chat when we came out of the Court and he told me that he had heard a rumour that Sam Allardyce, the then manager of Blackpool was interested in signing him and could I ring Sam on his behalf? I explained to Darren that I was not an agent and he should ring Sam himself and sort his deal out. This is exactly what he did and Darren signed for Blackpool.

These events got me thinking and I made enquiries of the Football Association (FA) to see what was required to become a registered players' agent. The requirements were stringent and included a £100,000 bond lodged with a Swiss bank account by Fédération Internationale de Football Association (FIFA), the passing of an exam relating to FA/FIFA rules and regulations and a signed contract with each player represented of not longer than two years. However, solicitors were exempt from these regulations when acting in the capacity of a solicitor for a client. I then had a word with a couple of people I relied upon and trusted. Lee Power, who had started his career at Norwich City and then moved to Bradford City and then on to Posh had kept in touch with his mates from his Norwich City days, including the likes of Tim Sherwood, Chris Sutton and Ruel Fox. Lee and Tim had used the flamboyant agent Eric Hall in the past and they arranged for me to meet Eric and discuss my plan. Eric is very funny and entertaining and is only really interested in telling Eric Hall stories and repeating his quotes, such as, "I never take yes for an answer," or ,"Why have free kicks when you can get a couple of quid for them?" Let me say that I think he encouraged me and wished me good luck. I then spoke to Chris Turner, the former player, manager and the-then joint owner of Posh and he set up a meeting for me with an agent named Graham Smith, who was in partnership with Frank McLintoch and had been involved in the Teddy Sheringham transfer from Nottingham Forest to Tottenham Hotspur which had allegedly involved "a bung" to Brian Clough. Again, he was supportive but I do not think he thought I would make any progress.

Yes, professional football is a glamorous, exciting world but it is a world where those involved do not like outsiders. Why? As a general rule all the managers, coaches, scouts etc are former players, they all either know each other personally or know of each other. Professional football was then, as it still is today outside the Premier League, a very small community where there was a way of doing things, which did not always need to be scrutinised by outsiders or involve outsiders, particularly people who are under a duty to do things properly, like lawyers. Also, at this time the enormous amounts of money players and managers are now paid was not common and some managers and persons connected to them thought it their right to earn something extra out of transfer deals. Again, to explain how the system worked, professional football clubs, particularly outside the Premier League, were usually owned by a local businessman, who had made their fortune and had been life-long supporters of their local clubs. They would be heavily involved in running a successful business and would speak to the manager and chief executive or club secretary daily but only attend at the ground on match days. They would underwrite the club's finances but the ex-player, now manager would generally, with a budget (but no financial involvement himself), sort out the players' contracts and transfers in and out. The owner would generally trust the manager and rely on his judgment until he was sacked for poor results and then a new manager would come in and get rid of the previous manager's signings and get his own players in.

The rumours and allegations in the game as to how the system worked for some unscrupulous managers were as follows;

• The selling manager likes "a drink". The allegation in the Teddy Sheringham transfer from Nottingham Forest to Tottenham was that Brian Clough "needed a drink." A drink being £50,000. Therefore, the agents involved issued an invoice for £50,000, later amended to include VAT which was paid in cash. This money was then handed over by the agent to the manager at the selling club. The buying club gets the player, the selling club gets the fee and the selling manager gets his drink.

• The managers of United and City are big mates and they have known each other for years. United have a player that the City manager would like to buy and both managers agree he is worth £400,000. However, the manager of City says, "I will persuade my owners to pay £500,000 if you pay me £50,000 cash." The manager of United explains the deal to his owners. They are getting £50,000 more than the player is worth. In appreciation of the payment, the manager of City then gives to the manager of United part of his £50,000 in cash unbeknown to the owner of United. Both managers are happy and the loser and victim is the owner of City. However, the manager of City knows his results are poor and he will be getting the sack soon anyway.

- The manager of City has a tame agent who is his mate. He tells the agent who he wants to sign and to make sure he represents him either solely or jointly with the player's existing agent. The manager of City will then tell his owner that he must sign the player but that his agent wants a fee of £100,000. Reluctantly, the owner of City agrees, the deal goes through and the agent shares his fee with the manager of City.

There are and have been many variations on these bungs and scams and to actually prove what is happening and provide an audit trail is virtually impossible. That is why these practices have continued unabated for such a long period. Amazingly, the financial success of football, even outside the Premier League, has affected matters in a positive way as managers are now much better paid and therefore the incentives balanced against the risk of discovery have made these scams less attractive. In any event, against a background of the matters set out above and hostility towards perceived outsiders, particularly lawyers, I launched my career as a lawyer/football agent. Due to me being involved with Posh, I had an agreement that I would not act for any of their players without agreement as I did not want a conflict of interest between the club and player.

I knew well most of the then current Posh playing squad. I talked to them. They had all been at other clubs previously and had kept in touch with mates at those clubs. I then spoke to ex-Posh players who had moved on and some of them were helpful and introduced me to their new team mates. Lee Power and Aidy Boothroyd were particularly helpful. The actual legal content of the transfer or registration of a professional footballer's contract is very straightforward. The Premier League/Football League contract is a standard document which has been refined and varied over the years in discussions between the Premier League, Football League and Professional Footballers' Association. It is common sense and deals with the amount of pay, the duration of the contract, bonuses and increases for promotion, disciplinary matters and termination payments (if any). In talking to players and managers at various clubs, you generally get a feel for what level of weekly wage, signing-on fee and bonuses a club will pay and what fee, if any, they will pay to an agent. One of the problems, as in all walks of life, is that people tend to exaggerate when they are talking about their wages. I always made sure I got a copy of the player's existing contract when I took on representation for a player.

I was up and running, no £100,000 bond needed and in the pre and early season of 1997, I dealt with the moves of three Posh players the club wanted out and negotiated their contracts:

- Goalkeeper Jon Sheffield to Plymouth Argyle for £100,000. The Plymouth manager, Mick Jones, had been a player at Posh in the mid 1970s and he was a straightforward man to deal with.

- Central defender, Greg Heald, to Barnet for £140,000. The Barnet manager was an ex-Posh manager, John Still, and I knew him well and he is a very pleasant, fair man to deal with.

- Central defender, Mark Foran, to Crewe Alexandra for £50,000. The Crewe manager was Dave Gradi and he had an excellent well-deserved reputation.

So far, so good, but as I started to act for a wider range of players I perhaps did not foresee the problems and hostility on the horizon.

Aidy Boothroyd had been a journeyman right back and played for a number of clubs, including Bristol Rovers, Hearts and Mansfield. On Easter Monday 1997, he was playing for Posh against Notts County at Meadow Lane and was tackled by Shaun Derry and left with a broken leg. He was admitted to Queens Medical Centre in Nottingham and was given an injection to relieve the pain he was suffering. Unfortunately, the site of the injection became infected and Aidy never really played again. He concentrated on his coaching career which eventually led him to the Premier League as a manager of Watford and then on to Colchester United and Coventry City. Whilst he was recovering from his leg injury, he would coach my son Edward's under-fourteen team, Netherton. One evening when he was round for tea, he telephoned his mate, Ian Baraclough. Ian and Aidy had been at Mansfield Town together but Ian was having a fantastic season at Notts County, who were running away with the old Division Three (now League Two). We met and I got on well with Ian and I started circulating his name around clubs. At the end of March, out of the blue, I got a call from Ray Harford, who was then manager at Queens Park Rangers (QPR). They had recently been relegated from the Premier League and were keen to bring in quality players to regain their Premier League status. Ian and myself went down to Loftus Road and met with Ray Harford and the chief executive, Clive Berlin. This was a big club, offering my client big money on a long-term deal and an excellent opportunity for furthering his career. After a long negotiation, we agreed terms, including an excellent agent's fee paid in instalments over the duration of the contract. The only problem was that it would all be effective from 1 June and in the meantime, Ian had to see out his contract at Notts County. Sam Allardyce was the manager at Notts County and he was not at all happy that Ian, who, on my advice, had rejected the offer of a new contract offered by Notts County, was going to be available to another club without a fee. I spoke to Sam and he was not happy with me or the player. He told me that he had agreed a fee of £125,000 with Sheffield United and we had to get up to Bramall Lane immediately to talk to them. I spoke to Ian and we agreed we had to go and had nothing to lose. Steve Thompson was the manager of Sheffield United and he and Ian had played together at Lincoln City. We went into a very scruffy office, underneath the main stand at Bramall Lane. Steve was not a man for formalities or small talk and merely said, "It is your party, what do you want?" He did not really want to speak to Ian or try and sell the club and its facilities. They were clearly a big club like QPR trying to regain former glory in the Premier League. I explained to him the terms we were looking for but his offer fell well short of the QPR offer. We thanked him for his time and left. When the news got back to

Sam Allardyce, he immediately went on the offensive in the Nottingham Evening Post and he branded Ian as "greedy". The report went on, "You do not turn down Sheffield United lightly. I find it incredible to watch a player turn down a dream move. As far as I am concerned it is pure greed." Now, any employee in any other walk of life would not be branded as greedy for trying to get the best deal he could for him and his family at the age of twenty-seven years in a short career. Ian wanted the best deal at the highest level; what is wrong with that? In any event, QPR came in for Ian before the transfer deadline and paid a fee so everybody was happy and Ian went on to a very successful spell with his new club.

At the same time as this deal, I also dealt with ex-Posh player Gary Martindale in his move from Notts County to Rotherham and had very pleasant dealings with their manager, Ronnie Moore, and his assistant, John Breckin. I liked them both and our good relationship was to pay off for me later. I had kept in touch with John McGlashan, the witness in the Darren Bradshaw case and he also moved to Rotherham United. He told me of a young player they had called Earl Jean. He had scored a hat trick at Burnley on the last day of the season but the team had been relegated and he had not been offered a new contract. John gave me Earl's number and I spoke to him and asked if I could help him find a new club. He readily agreed. I got him a trial at Mansfield Town and then a permanent deal with Plymouth Argyle. Earl was from the Caribbean Island of St Lucia and he had been brought over to Portugal by an agent along with two Trinidadians, Clint Marcelle, who was playing for Barnsley in the Premier League, and Russell Latapy, who had played for Porto under Bobby Robson and then Boavista. Earl told me that Russell wanted an agent to get him a club in Britain and asked if I could help. I spoke with Russell and I got him fixed up almost immediately with Alex McLeish at Hibernian in the Scottish Premier League through an agent called John Viola. I subsequently went up to Easter Road regularly to see Russell playing. He would always be the last one out of the changing rooms and he would often invite me in whilst he was having a soak in the bath, a cigarette and a Budweiser. He was a huge success in Scotland and went on to play for Rangers and then manage Motherwell.

At this time, all the English players with West Indian backgrounds were checking their roots and requesting to play for the island of their parents' birth. Earl Jean was from St Lucia. Kenny Charlery, a Posh legend, who scored both goals in the play-off final against Stockport in 1992, was from East London but both his parents were from St Lucia. Another lad I had done a deal for, Warren Hackett, who had been at Mansfield and Barnet, also had parents from St Lucia. I was in Antigua watching the England cricket team being annihilated by the West Indian fast bowlers Courtney Walsh and Curtley Ambrose and then by batsman Viv Richards and so to have a break from the cricket I got a flight over to St Lucia to meet up with Earl, Kenny and Warren and watch their international match against Martinique in their equivalent of a European Nations Cup Qualifier. I enjoyed the game and went out for a drink with the lads and they introduced me to an Englishman named Peter Miller, who was now working for the St Lucia Football Association. Peter was very easy to get along with and he told me that he was organising a conference for the Caribbean Football Association. He asked if I would like to come along in about a month as a guest speaker to talk about being a football agent and what it involved. I jumped at the opportunity, particularly as the venue was at the all inclusive Club St Lucia with all expenses paid.

I duly arrived about one month later as organised. All the British West Indies islands had sent a representative to the conference, from the big islands of Jamaica and Trinidad to the smaller islands of St Vincent and Monserrat. Peter Miller had made good contacts with Neil Warnock and Terry Robinson who were then respectively manager and chief executive of Bury. They were to take on the particular aspects of their work and Terry was, I believe, an FA councillor. They were good people and we had a great time, except that Neil seemed to be worried all the time about his new wife and baby and asked me to keep getting him drinks because his wife did not approve of him drinking alcohol whilst he was looking after his baby. At the end of what was a very successful conference, Peter Miller told me he was moving on to be the chief executive of a club in Trinidad called W Connection. Trinidad had the only full-time professional league in the Caribbean and there was much more scope for developing talent and introducing the best of it into the

UK. After about a year, once he had become established, Peter Miller invited me out to Trinidad to speak at another conference; this time with the former chief executive of the FA, Graham Kelly, whom I knew from my involvement with Posh, also because he lived just outside Peterborough in a village called Folksworth. The conference was nowhere near as good as the St Lucia conference but I made some useful contacts, including meeting up with Jack Warner, who was to become a member of the FIFA panel that decided on Russia as the venue for the 2018 World Cup and who has subsequently resigned his position with FIFA as a result of allegations of financial irregularities. Also in Trinidad at the time was Terry Fenwick, the former Tottenham and QPR defender who was playing for England when Maradona scored the infamous "hand of God" goal in the 1986 Mexico World Cup. He was manager of one of the local teams in the professional league. Ian Williamsfield was also present, the scorer of the Sunderland winning goal in the 1973 FA Cup final against Leeds United, and former manager of Chelsea who was now manager of the Trinidad national team. It was a good trip and useful contacts were made.

Shortly after I returned, Peter Miller got on to me about a Trinidad international striker called Stern John who was playing Major League Soccer in the USA for a team called Columbus Crew. Peter had done a good job and he had got Sir Bobby Robson at Newcastle United very interested. Peter had nominated me as his representative in the UK and he told me that Sir Bobby had my number and would be calling me, which he duly did. What a nice, polite, professional man. He explained to me that Newcastle United were appreciative for highlighting this player to them but they had nobody available to go to the USA to make contact with the player on their behalf and would I go? I did not need asking twice! They gave me a letter of authority on Newcastle United headed paper and paid for all my flights, food and accommodation to fly to Chicago and then on to Columbus to watch Columbus Crew versus Tampa Bay Mutiny in the MLS play-offs. The game was, in reality, very low-key with only about fourteen thousand people there. The star for Tampa Bay Mutiny was the Colombian International, Carlos Valderama, the one with the big orange afro. Columbus won 2-0 with Stern John scoring both, clearly having pace and an eye for goal.

I arranged to meet with Stern and his agent, a lawyer called Culpepper, originally from Trinidad but now based in Chicago. It was clear from the outset that they had already had discussions with other English clubs, particularly with David Platt at Nottingham Forest through Platt being good friends with Dwight Yorke from their old days at Aston Villa together. I arranged a second meeting but Stern and his agent did not have courtesy to turn up or make any excuses - they just left me waiting at the hotel. I returned home and did a full report for Sir Bobby and spoke to him on the phone. A short while later, Stern John signed for Nottingham Forest and went on to have quite a long career in England for a number of clubs.

By this time, I had been involved in a number of deals and was confident that I had a good phone book of managers' mobile numbers and had respect from most but there were exceptions. A young striker, called Kevin Rapley who was at Brentford, got in touch and asked if I would represent him. He felt he had got in the first team and was doing well and was worth a new contract and more money. Would I speak to the manager, Micky Adams on his behalf? I agreed. I did not know Micky Adams and had never had any dealings with him. I eventually got through to him and explained who I was. "Yes, what do you want?" Adams barked down the telephone. I explained politely, I thought, what Kevin had told me. He said, "Glen, (his assistant manager, Glen Cockerill) I have got some joker on the phone here asking for a pay increase for Raps." He then said to me, "Tell Raps he is lucky he has got a f★★★★ing contract and he is not getting more money." He then put the phone down. I thought the whole tone of the conversation and his attitude was totally inappropriate and this was one of the few occasions when I was treated with a total lack of respect, which was very disappointing but probably said more about Micky Adams than anything else.

I had built up some good contacts at Plymouth Argyle, although it was a long way from where I was based. I knew that Sam Allardyce at Notts County was interested in a lad named Chris Billy. I sent him a circular giving the player's details and rang him. "Sam, I am ringing about Chris Billy. Are you interested?" "Yes I am, but you are not his agent, Mark Curtis is," Sam replied. I knew there was no point in continuing the discussion. Mark Curtis handled a number of transactions at Notts County and then Bolton, Newcastle and other clubs where Sam was manager. Sam's son, Craig Allardyce, worked for him for a while. I had absolutely no legal cause for complaint about Chris Billy and I believe he did sign for Notts County. Mark Curtis is an interesting character and later represented Sam Allardyce in his own negotiation for management appointments. In January 1999, Allardyce sold Jermaine Pennant from Notts County to Arsenal. Subsequently, Mark Curtis was fined £7,500 and ordered to pay £10,000 costs by the FA and he was found guilty of four charges, including paying £700.00 to Pennant's father at an M25 service station and attempting to represent Pennant when he already had an agent. Further controversy concerned Curtis and Craig Allardyce when they worked together on deals involving Bolton Wanderers, where Sam was manager. Some of these deals were dealt with in a BBC Panorama documentary and The Quest Investigation carried out by Lord Stevens into thirty-nine Premier League transfers, nicknamed "The Bung Enquiry" in the media. Mike Newell, who had been manager at Luton Town, spoke out very surprisingly and bravely, claiming that corruption was rife throughout football. A number of transactions involving Luton Town were subject to complaint, including the transfer of Steve Howard for which Curtis received a payment of £18,000 and then an undeclared supplemental payment of £16,000. Curtis represented a large number of high profile players in high profile transfers and must have made a lot of fees from his work. I noticed in the newspaper the other day that the long-time representative of former Newcastle and now Liverpool striker, Andy Carroll, a man named Peter Harrison, is reporting fellow agent, Mark Curtis, claiming he has poached his client.

By contrast, I represented a goalkeeper called Phil Whitehead who had had a very successful career to date at Oxford United but it was now time for him to move on. There was a lot of interest in him and we arranged to meet with Tony Pulis at Bristol City in the morning and then drive on to the Madjewski Stadium in Reading to meet with Alan Pardew and John Gorman. Tony Pulis was polite, courteous and businesslike and made a very fair offer and the team were well placed for promotion to the Premier League. Phil liked

Tony Pulis and everything about the club and was keen to sign. I told him we had agreed to talk to Reading and we should follow it through. He agreed. The Madjewski Stadium, Alan Pardew and John Gorman were very impressive. They were not at that stage in a play-off position but the whole club was clearly primed for success. They told us Phil was not allowed to leave the stadium unless he signed a contract. This created a real dilemma. The money was about the same but the football was not as good at this stage. After four hours, Phil signed and we had to ring Tony Pulis with the news. He took it well.

I decided the best way to try and get representation of players in demand would be to contact such players direct. This approach was quite successful and I wrote to a couple of strikers who had always scored goals but who were out of contract that summer. Both strikers were originally from Scotland but now playing in England - Andy Thomson at Southend United and Allan Smart at Carlisle. Both players contacted me as a result of my letters to them and agreed that I could represent them. I soon got Andy Thomson fixed up at Oxford United, who were then in Division One (now the Championship) and managed by their former player, Malcolm Shotton. Andy went on to have a successful spell there for himself and then moved onto Gillingham where again things went well for him and he scored a few goals and they were promoted in the play-offs. Initially, with Allan Smart, Northampton Town were very keen and we had a meeting at their Sixfields Stadium with their chairman and they made a very good offer which seemed about right and the player was keen to accept. However, a couple of days before we had to make a decision, I got a call out of the blue from the former England manager, Graham Taylor, who was back at Watford and they were pushing for promotion to the Premier League. Allan, Graham Taylor, his then assistant Kenny Jackett and I had a long discussion and sorted out a financial deal. Allan had suffered injury problems in the past but he managed to pass the medical. He was a real success for Watford and scored the winning goal in the play-off final at the end of the following season and then had one season in the Premier League before unfortunately Watford were relegated.

The most disappointing deal I was involved in was that of Ian Richardson from Notts County to Wimbledon, who were then still in the Premiership. A substantial fee was agreed. We had discussions with the player and the Wimbledon chairman at his offices in Central London and negotiated a fantastic deal for the player and a £25,000 agent's fee for me payable by Wimbledon. The only outstanding issue was the medical examination. Everybody was really happy and I was really pleased for Ian, who came into the game later in his career via Barry Fry at Birmingham City. What happened? Yes, he failed his medical. That was the end of the deal and Ian stayed on at Notts County.

Two deals which gave me the most pleasure were young lads going from non-league teams to Premiership teams: the stuff dreams are made of. The first was a Peterborough lad called Mark Paul, who transferred from Kings Lynn to then Premiership side Southampton for £100,000. David Jones was the Southampton manager and Mark immediately became part of the first team squad with players such as Matthew Le Tissier, Mark Hughes and Carlton Palmer. Unfortunately, Mark never adjusted. Whether he was home sick or he did not develop as expected, I do not know but it did not work out. He was on £500.00 per match appearance for the first team. He made the bench once as an unused sub and then just drifted downwards and ended up back at non-league clubs in the Peterborough area. The second deal worked out well. David Norris was another Peterborough lad who, from the Lord Westwood pub team in Peterborough Sunday Morning League, moved on to Stamford and then Boston. Bolton Wanderers, managed by my old adversary, Sam Allardyce, agreed a fee of £100,000 for David and we sorted out personal terms on a Friday evening at the Marriott Hotel, Huntingdon on the eve of an FA Cup tie they had with Cambridge United. Sam and his assistant, Phil Brown, were perfect gentlemen and the deal was quickly tied up. David struggled to break through at Bolton and then had a very successful spell at Plymouth Argyle before moving to Ipswich Town for £2.5 million and then Portsmouth. Everybody agrees he works hard and is a lovely lad.

Ian Moore, the son of Rotherham manager Ronnie Moore, was recommended to me by his father. Ian had had a good career and

Nottingham Forest had paid £1 million in 1997 for him before he found himself scoring a lot of goals at Stockport County in the old Division One (now the Championship). Stockport wanted to cash in on Ian and agreed a fee with Norwich City and Burnley and we arranged to discuss personal terms with both clubs on consecutive days. We met with Norwich City representatives, including then manager Bryan Hamilton, at a hotel in Birmingham. Norwich's results on the field were poor. They were not scoring enough goals. Ian was a northern lad with a family. Norwich is a fantastic city but a long way from everywhere except Ipswich. Ian was not keen. Norwich had a budget which was lower than our expectations. Bryan Hamilton became very annoyed with the way negotiations had gone and he was shouting and banging on the table. The reality was that Ian did not want to sign for Norwich City. I had never seen this sort of conflict before and it was clear we were never going to sort out a deal. The next day we met with the Burnley chairman at his office in Blackburn. Stan Ternent was the Burnley manager. He was bright, chirpy and cheerful and when he saw the deal Ian had been offered by the chairman, asked if could borrow some money off him if he got short! Everybody was happy and the deal concluded. Ian had a long spell at Burnley.

By about 2005, I was beginning to think football agency was hard work. More and more people were becoming FIFA registered and players and clubs were becoming wiser themselves and playing the agents off against each other. The big players; Rooney, Terry, Beckham, Lampard, all have agents who deal with all their activities. The agents are well-established and generally good at what they do. As we all know, there had then been a tremendous influx of players, mainly into the Premier League, but in the lower leagues as well, from overseas. These players often had agents from their country of origin in South America, Eastern Europe or Africa. In addition, many top managers and club owners were from overseas and they had their existing contracts that they were comfortable to deal with. In reality, this left the not so successful Premier League players plus the lower leagues and young players coming through as the market for English based agents. In addition to these changes, more and more people were passing their FIFA exams and becoming registered agents or using the loophole I had used and acting as a solicitor or on behalf of a solicitor in representing players. It is also important to understand the mentality of footballers. Aidy Boothroyd always said to me, "Footballers are generally just ordinary working class blokes who had a particular ability to kick a ball and make a living from it." They received no more or less training in social skills, accountancy or politeness, than any other members of their peer group. Consequently, when faced with decisions and engaged with people, some players struggle. At most clubs there are usually two or three influential players who, in reality, decide what agents to use, where to get your car repaired, what restaurant to eat at and what bars and clubs to go to. Usually, these services are provided fairly locally to the club by supporters caught up in the glamour and at no charge. As, by this time, I had already lost or was losing my connections with Posh and the owners of professional football clubs and the players I knew well were getting older and drifting out of the game, I was finding it harder and harder to get players to represent that were of reasonable quality and were loyal. Players I spoke to would say "I have spoken to a number of agents and I am not signing with any one of them but if you get me a move, I will go with you." This was an impossible situation as you could spend hours establishing if a club was interested in a particular player and then if the club made a move the player would be free at that stage to choose whatever agent he wanted and exclude you from the deal after hours of time and trouble. Also, quite understandably, many managers did not want to commit to a player until they had got other players out or had sorted out funding with their chairman. In the past, I had always put up with the problem and had some really successful deals on the basis of "Get me the move and I will go with you," but these deals were getting harder to find.

Another problem with players is that they had always heard a rumour from a "good source" that the likes of Manchester United or Arsenal want to sign. You can spend hours trying to get through to Sir Alex Ferguson or Arsene Wenger and when you do get through they say they are not interested. Players who are not currently in the team are another major problem and would get on to me and say, "Can you ring the manager and ask him why I am not in the team?" In reality, we all know the answer and Chris Turner at Posh always said to players sarcastically, "Think about it mate, you are not in the team because you are the best player we have got!" I have never met a professional, or for that matter an amateur footballer, who has underestimated his own ability. The converse of the above is players who break into the team and do well and, say, score a couple of goals. They then want you to call the manager and renew their contract, which in reality is never going to happen. Hours are spent discussing the matter and if you refuse to do it, they want a new agent! The last deal I did was when Brett Omerod moved from Southampton and was signed by Billy Davis for Preston North End in 2006. My illness and a couple of other factors conspired and that was the end of an era where I met fantastic people, travelled to fantastic places and got to know professional football inside out. Do I miss it? No. Well, perhaps a bit!

9. *Mad Hatters*

Ever fancied doing a live interview on a Sunday morning on BBC Radio Five Live or Sky Sports? How about being quoted on football matters in The News of the World, The Mirror, The Mail and even The Observer? I did all these things but, in my case, none of the publicity was a pleasure, more like an ordeal. We all make mistakes in life and my good mate, Lee Power and I made a huge mistake when we agreed to assist a consortium of property developers take over Luton Town Football Club, nicknamed "The Hatters."

I had known Peter Miller for years and had had dealings with him through my football agency when he had been based in St Lucia and Trinidad in the West Indies. He had then moved back to England and got a job as Chief Executive of Northampton Town Football Club. Peter was very friendly with former Tottenham Hotspur, QPR and England defender, Terry Fenwick, who had been involved in club management in Trinidad. I got to know Terry through Peter and he was a nice fellow. Lee Power and I got on well with both Peter and Terry. Lee was also involved as a director at Northampton Town and for a short while Terry was manager. Terry had a number of England caps as a central defender and he was one of the England defenders trying to stop Argentina's Diego Maradona scoring the "hand of god" goal and his subsequent brilliant individual goal in the 1986 Quarter Final of the World Cup in Mexico. From his playing days, Terry knew a businessman called

John Gurney. I knew nothing about John Gurney and as things turned out, I should have done some homework.

Peter got on to Lee and myself and explained he was going to be part of a consortium of property developers who wanted to take over Luton Town Football Club. The consortium was fronted by John Gurney and the money was coming from the Far East and South Africa. The plan was to relocate the football club to a new site just off one of the M1 motorway exits and to develop the old Kenilworth Road ground for housing or industrial purposes. The consortium had no interest whatsoever in football matters and they wanted Peter to be the Chief Executive, Terry to be the Manager and Lee and myself to be the Chairman and Vice Chairman and to oversee the running of the football side of the business and the sale and purchase of players. Since I left Peterborough United, I had been looking for an opportunity to get back into football and be involved in the running of a club. The proposal seemed a wonderful idea.

Lee and myself had a couple of meetings with Peter, Terry and John Gurney at hotels near Luton and then at the Kenilworth Road football ground. John Gurney was quite a mysterious man. He described himself as a businessman but never revealed what type of business he was in or what he had done in the past, other than "property development." Everywhere he went, he was accompanied by a very attractive lady of Chinese origin in her mid-twenties, described as his personal assistant (PA). John talked a big game of large all-seater stadiums and millions of pounds. He had apparently already done the deal with the existing Luton Town shareholders and directors. Peter Miller had signed a letter terminating the positions of Joe Kinnear and Mick Harford as team managers. Little did we realise that Peter had sacked the most popular management team at Luton Town in recent seasons. The sacking was unpopular and guaranteed to produce a backlash from the supporters. However, as far as Lee and I were concerned the sacking of the existing football management team was not important and the plan all fitted together. Terry Fenwick was to be the new Team Manager, Peter Miller the new Chief Executive, Lee Power, the new Vice Chairman and I was to be the new Chairman. John Gurney's PA had organised a press conference for just Lee and me in the boardroom at Kenilworth

Road the next day to make all the exciting announcements relating to the new structure of the club. So far, so good, and I believe we were due at the club between 1.30pm and 2.00pm.

The roads leading to the main entrance at Kenilworth Road are not particularly easy to negotiate and consist of Victorian terraced houses and a number of one way narrow streets with cars and other vehicles parked all over the place. Lee and I met up before we got to the ground and Lee had borrowed his mate's new black S class Mercedes and really looked the part. I was also driving a Mercedes and as we drove through the narrow streets and up to the main entrance, we could not help but see a heavy police presence and what was later estimated as two or three hundred people being held back at the entrance to the ground by the police. We parked our cars next to each other and as we walked across the car park to the entrance, the baying mob was hurling not only abuse at us but also bottles and eggs. We hurried across the car park and into the main entrance, both shocked and worried by the hostility we had encountered. We were ushered up to the boardroom where John Gurney's PA was waiting and also the club secretary, Cherry Newbery, whom I had known previously from my Peterborough United days and who was well respected in football circles.

Cherry obviously had a lot of local knowledge and she explained to us that the supporters were really upset as Joe Kinnear and Mick Harford were successful and popular and they had been sacked for no good reason. In addition, nobody knew anything about the property consortium or what their plans were and for the first time we had appeared as their public face. The supporters were angry with the secrecy and lack of communication about their beloved club and what was going to happen with it. There were a number of unofficial websites that had generated speculation and anger. The Bedfordshire Police Inspector in charge of policing outside the ground came into the boardroom to see us. He explained that if we left matters too long before we left the stadium he could not guarantee our safety. Word was spreading on mobile phones and the internet that we were at the ground and more and more angry supporters were turning up waiting to vent their hostility towards the representatives of the consortium. That was Lee and I!

All the local football media and some nationals were outside the boardroom waiting to hear from us. It was decision time for Lee and I. What were we going to do? We were football people and had no involvement whatsoever in property development or the sacking of the existing manager and his assistant. The supporters were hostile and that hostility was directed towards us as the representatives of the consortium. We both agreed we did not need the aggravation and we would have to reconsider our position. The press, the radio and television crews were there waiting to hear from us. We decided we had no choice but to do the interviews. The media were ushered into the boardroom and they set up their cameras and microphones. We explained to the journalists and TV and radio reporters exactly what our position was and that we were football people. We were only interested in running the football side of the business and the sales and purchases of players. We were not property developers and due to the level of hostility we had encountered we would be reconsidering our proposed appointment as Chairman and Vice Chairman of Luton Town Football Club. Lee is one of the most chirpy, cheerful, jokey characters that you will ever meet but if you look at the photographs taken in the boardroom on that day, you can see the look of total despair and possibly fright on his face as he anticipated our reception from the supporters waiting outside the stadium. In the end I believe the media representatives felt sorry for us. In any event, they had got their stories and photographs so they were not really worried about our fate.

The press conference finished and the Police Inspector came back and told us that we should leave immediately for our own safety. We should go to our cars and drive out through the main entrance. His officers would hold back the baying crowd and hopefully make a path so we could drive straight out of the ground without stopping or stalling. We left the boardroom and walked out of the main entrance to our cars, escorted by police officers. As soon as the baying crowd spotted us, the abuse, bottles and eggs started coming our way. We agreed Lee would leave first in his car and I would follow immediately behind him. The police officers protecting us radioed their colleagues holding back the crowd. The gates of the car park opened and we drove out. As we got to the narrowing of the road, where the crowd was, they surged forwards and I saw bottles hitting Lee's car and heard them hitting my car. The crowd were also trying to force their way through the police cordon and were kicking out at both cars. We both managed to get past the mob without stalling and down the road where fortunately there were no parked cars in the way and the traffic lights were green. We had escaped without physical injury but also without enhancing our reputation. The next day I spoke to Lee and he had £500.00 worth of damage to the S class, however, as we had escaped we could have a laugh about our very unpleasant ordeal.

June is a very quiet time for football news and we made all the football headlines for all the wrong reasons. We did not proceed with our appointments and nor did Peter and Terry. Joe Kinnear and Mick Harford were reappointed as manager and assistant manager. I believe the takeover by the consortium did not take place. We subsequently discovered that John Gurney had been involved in various proposals to take over football and rugby clubs for property developers and that three years previously he had been acquitted of involvement in a £100 million drug smuggling case. I believe he was subsequently made bankrupt and I do not know what he is up to now. Lee and I were required to give statements to Bedfordshire Police as one of us ran over the foot of the Inspector involved in keeping the crowd back when we made our swift exit and there was a surge forward. The moral of the story is that not all publicity is good and you should do your homework on business ventures where your reputation is on the line. With hindsight, Lee and I often laugh about being Chairman and Vice Chairman of Luton Town for one day!

10. *I Will Never Be Ill and Immortality*

My mother, father, brother and sister have very luckily always enjoyed good health. My father has continued working into his ninety-sixth year and was featured in The Farmers' Weekly as Britain's oldest grain trader. As children, we were never allowed to be ill and never had a day off school. As a result of this upbringing, I never had any time off school or work, our family did not get ill, and I was totally unsympathetic with people who were ill.

All was to change. My wife booked a fantastic six week holiday for us, touring around the North and South Islands of New Zealand. We were due to go in February. A few days before we were due to go, I was not feeing well and my tonsil on the left side of my neck was swollen. I had suffered from tonsillitis in the past and thought I had tonsillitis again. I went to see my GP and told him the symptoms and then did my usual trick; I self-diagnosed and said to the GP, "I've got tonsillitis." He looked down my throat and said there was definitely something wrong and shook his head. He did not disagree with my self-diagnosis, prescribed me some antibiotics and said if the symptoms did not improve to come back and see him on my return from holiday.

Whilst I was away, the symptoms persisted and quite a large lump developed on my left tonsil. Even I was concerned as this was not like the tonsillitis I had previously experienced. A couple of days after I returned home I went back to my GP. He examined me and looked down my throat again and started shaking his head. He called in his colleague from the consulting room next door who also examined me and they began to talk as if I was not there and they began shaking their heads and tutting. They finally apologised and said they were sorry but they believed I had a fairly well advanced cancerous growth on my left tonsil and must have an immediate consultation with an ear, nose and throat (ENT) surgeon and an oncologist. I was absolutely stunned, shocked and worried. Me, who was never going to be ill, with throat cancer; it was not possible!

I walked back to my office, which was only five minutes away and my head was spinning. What is going on? What is throat cancer? What is the treatment? Is it terminal? Am I going to die? In these dreadful circumstances, the human mind really does go into overdrive and goes into areas that you would prefer that it did not – how will the family cope? What about finances? Five minutes later when I arrived back at the office, I asked my wife Cherry to come up to my room and I outlined to her what had happened and the discussion at the GP's surgery. She was cool and calm as usual and gave me the advice that I always try and give to people in these types of difficult circumstances – do not go too far out; take it one step at a time; wait and see the outcome of the tests and the diagnosis. I worried about all these issues over the weekend and did not sleep well.

Monday arrived and I attended at the Fitzwilliam Hospital in Bretton, Peterborough and met with Mr Bhat the Consultant Surgeon. He was and is a very impressive man with an excellent patient manner and he put me at ease to a certain extent, explaining that there needed to be urgent tests, scans and biopsies. I immediately started the long process of intrusive tests and examinations and because of the potential seriousness of the condition, all tests and examinations were carried out as emergencies – this cancerous growth on my tonsil was growing daily and the possibility of it spreading to other areas was very real.

After the tests I went back to work pending the results but as you may imagine, my concentration levels were not good and I was more irritable and impatient than normal. I did not really want to discuss the situation with anyone except for family and close friends because I did not have the results of the tests and I did not really know what was happening and the treatment involved. By the end of the week I received a telephone call from the Fitzwilliam Hospital arranging an appointment to discuss the results of the tests. My wife Cherry came along to the appointment with me. I was very nervous and apprehensive as I was ushered into the consulting room to be met by a smiling Mr Bhat and his Oncologist colleague. They were obviously very experienced in breaking life threatening and life changing news to their patients. They did not beat about the bush and told me straight. Firstly, Mr Bhat told me that I had a stage two cancerous growth on my left tonsil. I knew what cancer meant but what was stage two? I was informed that the stage cancers have reached are defined using a scale of one to four, with four being the most serious. I would have to have immediate surgery to remove the cancerous growth on my left tonsil and also to remove the adjacent lymph nodes into which some cancer may have spread. In layman's terms, they would have to remove the cancer but also the surrounding good cells and associated tissue on the basis that whilst I was opened up, they had to make sure that they were getting rid of the total problem rather than just taking away the minimum and then having to return for more intrusive surgery at a later stage. Obviously, the throat and neck are very complex and delicate areas of the body with a lot of important functions going on. I half expected the diagnosis and although stunned, I still tried to understand the seriousness of the surgery and what would happen next. Again, although we like to be optimistic, the pessimistic side of the brain also has questions and I did have to ask what would happen if the cancer had spread from the tonsil. No problem said Mr Bhat, we would just have to carry out further surgery and remove further damaged cells and tissue including my tongue and voice box. Before I could ask a further question, Mr Bhat told me that my tongue could then be rebuilt with muscle (I think) from my thigh and my voice box could be reconstructed - from where and how I did not question. I could then be taught how to talk again. This was one of those occasions where I perhaps wished I had not asked the question as I definitely did not like the answer.

Mr Bhat's colleague, Dr Benson, the Oncologist, then explained to me the treatment I would be subjected to very shortly after I had recovered from the surgery. Due to the risk of the cancer spreading, this would only be three or four weeks later. I would have to have a six week course of radiotherapy. I stopped listening at this stage and although I was being very helpfully told what to expect, the words did not register with me except the final words of, "It will be tough." I had lots of questions to ask but I was in a state of shock and asked "What are the chances that the treatment will be a success?" "Fifty-fifty," was the response and then the arrangements were made for the surgery to take place in two days time. For someone like me who was paid to talk as part of this job and in any event talked too much, this was devastating news. Many things we are told or news we are given throughout our lives causes us a certain level of upset and distress but the news I had just received took this level of upset to a new dimension. Inevitably, you go through in your own mind what you have achieved in life and the things you would still like to achieve, the places you would like to travel to, your children's weddings and grandchildren. The fragility of our existence really hits home and everyday worries which we all have, many of which are financial, become totally insignificant and you would give everything you have materially and financially to have good health. Anyway, how could I have throat cancer? I had never smoked and it was normally associated with smokers. What can you do? Just get on with it. There is no choice. I am not brave but I am compliant. Two days later I turned up for my major throat surgery. What would the effect of the operation be? Would it be a success? Should I start planning my funeral?

I do not know how long the operation lasted but anyway, I woke up and the nurse gave me a mirror to look at the thirty two staples which had been inserted instead of stitches to seal the wound together. Surprisingly, I did not feel too bad but I was having strong doses of painkillers including morphine. At this stage the treatment was physical and I am a good healer. I was in hospital for a few days and had my wife and children and other friends and relatives visiting and I did not feel too bad at all. After I was discharged I even went into work and drafted a few letters and documents. Little did I realise, my ordeal was just beginning and the worst was just about to begin.

Addenbrookes Hospital is in Cambridge on a huge site consisting of randomly arranged buildings but has an international reputation for treatment of various medical conditions including throat and neck cancers. Initially I was attending to have a plaster cast taken of my head and neck. This plaster cast is then used as a mould to make a perspex mask. The idea of the perspex mask is that when you lay on what is like a metal bench to have radiotherapy treatment, the mask is bolted over your face so that you do not move as the area of the neck to be treated must be very specifically targeted. Radiotherapy rays are very dangerous and can cause collateral damage to other parts of the body if this process is not adopted. I was to have radiotherapy treatment every working day for six weeks. I had been told by the oncologist that it would be "tough" but I had to be determined and I would get through it. One of the side effects of the surgery and radiotherapy was that I would not be able to chew, swallow or eat for up to six months. Therefore, I would have to have a plastic tube surgically inserted into my stomach and then be taught how to plug this into an electronic pump which would feed me with a liquid glucose type feed and deliver to me all the necessary vitamins and nutrients etc that I would normally get from food. The tube was fitted in a surgical procedure and I was shown how to work the pump and given a knapsack so that I could walk around with the pump working.

Two weeks after the surgery, the chemotherapy and radiotherapy started. Chemotherapy was at the Nuffield Hospital in Cambridge and was administered by an absolutely fantastic nursing team. The treatment involved being plugged into an intravenous drip and having two hours of water flushed through your system, two hours of chemotherapy and then another two hours of water. It was a long day, and then I had to go off for radiotherapy treatment which fortunately only lasted for about thirty minutes.

You can never be prepared for the side effects and the total general debility that chemotherapy gives; a total feeling of lethargy, nausea, constipation, aching, and no desire for days to do anything except sleep or sit in a chair in front of the television, not necessarily watching it but just having it on for company. I was not allowed to drive and every day I still had to arrange for my very best, closest friends to take me from my home in Peterborough to Addenbrookes for radiotherapy treatment. The journey was about one hour each way and the treatment only lasted about thirty minutes.

After about six weeks, the effects of the treatment and feeding through a stomach pump were really getting to me. I had so much pain in my throat due to the radiotherapy treatment. The effect was like sunburn on the exterior of my skin but also a continually sore throat and thirst. Even worse, I lost my voice and could only communicate via handwritten notes. By this time, I was having very strong doses of morphine. I must admit that I did like the effect of the morphine as it took away the pain completely but not without side effects – morphine friends. One evening I was sitting in our living room with my wife watching television. I had just had a very strong dose of morphine. I asked my wife who all the people were sitting with us in our living room. I could see at least ten people watching television with us. They were not rude or speaking, they just sat there. Cherry said, "What are you talking about? There is only me and you in the room." I then realised that "seeing things" was one of the side effects of strong morphine doses.

After eight weeks treatment, the chemotherapy and radiotherapy finally came to the end that I never thought I would reach. I slowly got my voice back but still could not eat solid food. The morphine doses stopped but I now have some insight into the effect of opiate based drugs, as I could not keep still for a period of about two weeks. I would twitch and walk about. This was a side effect of the morphine slowly working its way out of my system.

Very slowly, my health started to improve. I started back at work and got back into going to court and presenting cases on behalf of clients. I was still not eating properly and feeding myself via the pump which I would often plug in if I was going on a car journey. I remember on one occasion, I was coming back from Bedford County Court after a child contact hearing and the client was travelling in my car with me. Disaster struck and the pump malfunctioned and covered me in the sticky glucose feed. It was so embarrassing but the client was very understanding and helped me clear up the mess. Perhaps I was being too ambitious and I should have just succumbed to the treatment.

I was continually tested and scanned to make sure the treatment was still effective and there was no spreading of the cancer to other areas. After six months, I was able to start eating again and I did not have to use the tube. Slowly, slowly, I was getting back to health. I was back at work and I was having physiotherapy to build up the strength in the left side of my body, which the surgery had damaged. My throat was continually sore and my speech and hearing had been affected by the treatment. One of the worst side effects for me was that I could not eat and enjoy spicy food, as my taste buds had been damaged and anything slightly spicy or hot would cause too much pain to eat. No more chicken madras for me!

Life gradually got back to normal but I was regularly monitored as I was still at risk. I had the scars and was coming to terms with the side effects, particularly the continued dryness and soreness in the mouth. About two years after the surgery, I remember having a routine chest x-ray. Quite a few weeks passed and I thought no more of it and went off on holiday with my wife to Sardinia. We had a wonderful break, eating and drinking far too much as usual.

When we returned home from holiday, there was an urgent message from Mr Bhat, the consultant that had carried out the original surgery and was supervising my recovery. The x-rays which I had had taken a few weeks ago had got lost between the hospital and my GP and nobody had looked at them. When eventually the x-rays turned up and they were examined, they revealed a shadow, which to the expert eye looked like another cancerous growth and I would have to come in immediately for more tests. The same thought crossed my mind as it had with the throat cancer. How could I have lung cancer? Only smokers got lung cancer. After the surgery and deliberating treatment I had been through, I was totally deflated. I made an appointment with Mr Bhat and went to see him at his clinic. He apologised for the mix up with the x-rays and told me I could make a formal complaint if I wished. "What is the point?" I thought. There was inevitably a delay but the problem was the cancer, not complaining about hospital staff not doing their job properly. I was subjected to more x-rays, biopsies, scans etc but the diagnosis was as feared: a totally unrelated tumour on my right lung. I was dispatched off to see another oncologist who specialised in these matters. This time, it was Mr Gillespie at Papworth Hospital near Cambridge. At first I was subjected to all types of heart and lung function tests to establish my lung capacity and fitness for the forthcoming surgery. My fitness levels were good. I then had the consultation with Mr Gillespie and he explained that I would have one of the three lobes of my right lung removed and hopefully this would remove all traces of the tumour and we would all have to hope it had not spread elsewhere. Again, I was shocked, upset and all of the other emotions that I had experienced before. The oncologist reassured me for what it was worth by telling me that many people survive with just one lung. I thought fine, no problem, but I did not want to be that person.

I remember going down to Papworth Hospital near Cambridge on the day before the operation. Of course, all the hospital staff were very positive, helpful and sympathetic but I was really worried about the effect of having one third of my right lung removed. How would I breathe? Would I still be able to walk any distance? Would I need a wheelchair or walking sticks? Again, the human mind was taking me where I did not want to go. I was due to go down for my operation at 2.00pm. I was prepared by the nursing staff and given a pre-med, which relaxed me and I lay on the bed waiting for the theatre porter to come to wheel me down to the theatre. 2.30pm. 3.00pm. 3.30pm. Nobody had arrived. I was worried and nervous about the operation but nothing, no message, no communication from the hospital staff whatsoever. I wandered out from my room and asked the staff nurse what was happening. She said she did not know and she would find out but in the meantime I should be a patient patient. I have never been patient. I just wanted to know what was happening. 4.00pm. 5.00pm. At 6.00pm, the surgeon came into to see me, still wearing his theatre gown. He apologised profusely but explained they had had an emergency and they just had to deal with it. I was upset, angry and stressed that I had just wanted some communication rather than hanging around waiting for four hours for life changing surgery. The surgeon explained that it was now too late in the day to carry out the surgery but I would be first in the list the next day. By this time, Cherry had arrived to visit me and the surgeon agreed I could get dressed and go out for a meal and stay overnight at home, provided I was back by 9.00am the next morning. I agreed. The next morning I was there on time and the operation took place as planned. I remember waking up and realising the surgery had happened. How would I feel? Would I be able to breathe? Would I be short of breath? I took some large gulps of air and to my pleasant surprise I could breathe and I did not feel short of breath. I stayed in hospital for a few days and my family and all my loyal friends came to visit.

The rehabilitation was slow as the surgery was major and then I was back on for another course of chemotherapy at the Nuffield Hospital, administered in a very similar way by the same nurses. Again, the chemotherapy was very debilitating but there was no radiotherapy this time. The side effects caused me severe chest pains, to the extent that I ended up in casualty at Peterborough District Hospital one Friday night in the early hours with all the drunks and fight injuries from a standard Friday night. But slowly I recovered, and got back to work with regular visits to the oncologist at Papworth and the usual x-rays, tests and scans.

I have been told I am unlucky as it is extremely unusual for a person to suffer two completely unconnected cancerous tumours in different areas of the body. Whether I am unlucky, or lucky to be alive, I do not know, but one thing for sure is that I am much more sympathetic than I used to be when I come across anyone with illnesses or ailments. I hope that as a result of the extensive surgery, radiotherapy and chemotherapy, I am and will remain free of any reoccurrence or new cancers. My health has of course been severely affected by the treatment and in particular I have suffered a loss of taste, difficulty in swallowing and a continually sore and dry throat, which means I drink about fifteen cups of tea a day, which cannot be good for me. But I have been lucky with the professional medical treatment, I have recovered and have received tremendous practical support from my family and friends and my work colleagues.

★

I am a people person and I love characters. One of the advantages of being a solicitor is that we do come across all types of characters of all ages and from all walks of life. One such character who stands out is Jonathan Waller. He was a good friend of mine and a client as a result of his acrimonious divorce from his ex-wife

Sarah. Jon was a real "Jack-the-lad" and just could not resist a pretty girl (or sometimes not so pretty). He really did struggle to make lasting relationships, although he was desperate to find Ms Right and settle down.

Jon was always available if you needed someone to come to a football match, horse race, meeting or a party. Whatever, he was there, particularly if it was free. He did "own" an affinity marketing firm and because of his charm and personality he made excellent contacts with very influential people but unfortunately he would not always deliver and often let people down. He always portrayed a happy image and his "Jon Wallerisms" were, "You do not need to be a millionaire, you just need to live like one", "I will be there in five minutes", which meant he would be there in half an hour, and, "The railway barrier was down at Tallington" – this was the excuse for his lateness, but we soon worked out that he rarely came via Tallington. He doted on his daughter, Jodie, and always tried to exercise regular contact with her and shower her with love and affection (and presents). He also had another child from what he would describe as "a casual relationship" with a young woman who worked behind the counter in a betting office. Jon became very friendly with a Peterborough born-and-bred businessman named Phillip Carter. Phillip, in a very short time, built up a multi-million pound business empire. He had also acquired a well-known landmark hotel on the A1 near Stamford, known as The Haycock Hotel at Wansford and a massive stately home at Thornhaugh nearby. He had the expensive cars, the helicopter and the very exclusive season tickets at Chelsea Football Club.

In my experience, Jon had always been a Posh supporter but as his friendship with Phillip Carter developed, he seemed to be attending more and Chelsea games as Phillip Carter's guest and he also purchased season tickets himself for a nice executive area at the ground. Jon was then invited regularly by Phillip to attend Champions League fixtures, both home and away, and they regularly travelled in Phillip's Squirrel helicopter, with Phillip's seventeen year old son, Andrew.

Jon would never deal with mundane matters and after his divorce, I kept stressing to him that he should make a will to make proper provision in the event of an accident. Jon was like a lot of people – why would he need to make a will when he was immortal? He was never going to die, so why bother with a boring, mundane will? I knew how he wanted to provide for his children in the event of his death and sent him a draft will and asked him to come into the office to discuss matters further. No response. I sent him reminders. No response. In February 2007, Jon and I and some other friends had been away for a week's ski-ing to Kitzbuhel in Austria. We had a great time. Life was good for Jon; he had two or three women on the go as usual, and he was beginning to make some money in his business.

On the evening of Tuesday 2 May 2007, Chelsea were playing Liverpool in a Champions League semi-final being played at Anfield. I knew Jon was going to the game with Phillip Carter and his son. They were to travel to and from the game in Phillip's Squirrel helicopter from Phillip's house at Thornhaugh near Stamford to Liverpool John Lennon Airport and straight back home after the game. Jon had told me that previously he had had scary moments in the helicopter when it lost altitude rapidly on a couple of occasions, but Phillip just took the mickey out of him and said there was nothing to be scared of. This seemed to make sense, as Phillip was not going to put his life and his son's life at risk.

On the Wednesday morning, I got up early as I needed to be at Court in good time to deal with a complex financial case arising from the breakdown of a marriage with a very aggressive barrister on the other side. I sat having my breakfast and there was a report on the national news that a helicopter had left Liverpool the previous night and had been lost on radar screens. There was no sign that the helicopter had been located and the police and personnel from nearby RAF Wittering were searching. That news came as a shock to me as I knew Jon had travelled up to the game in Phillip Carter's helicopter and I just hoped they had crash landed somewhere and everyone was safe. I contacted my good friend and Jon's lodger, Simon Rusk (Rusky), and asked him what he knew. He said he would keep me informed.

During the morning, my phone was red hot but I could not take the calls as I was embroiled in this complex case and I probably did not have the best level of concentration at this stage. My case finally settled around lunchtime and I put my phone back on and nervously phoned Rusky. He told me that the wreckage of the helicopter had been found and that the pilot and the three passengers had not survived. I was absolutely stunned. I thanked Rusky and put the phone down. There was nothing to say. I read the eulogy at Jon's funeral in Market Deeping and attended the memorial service in Peterborough Cathedral for Phillip Carter. As you would imagine, both services were very well attended. Amazingly, within ten months of his death, Phillip Carter's company Carter & Carter had gone into administration and the shares were worthless. His holding at the date of his death was valued at £111 million. Despite my encouragement, Jon had not made his will and his estate was distributed in accordance with the Intestacy Rules, which is not what he wanted. The moral of the story is, as we all know in reality, none of us are immortal!

11. I Swear to Tell the Truth, What is in a Name and The Kama Sutra

Imagine the scene – North Cambridgeshire Family Proceedings Court, Bridge Street, Peterborough. We have a case issued by the father under the Children Act 1989 to have contact with his two year old daughter, who lives with his former partner, the child's mother. I am there, in Court, representing the mother and ready to begin my cross-examination of the father. The mother asserts there have been twenty four incidents of domestic violence perpetrated against her by the father whilst they were in a relationship. The father denies all twenty four incidents and the purpose of the court hearing is to establish the facts and who is telling the truth and, once the facts have been established, what impact these facts will have on the future contact arrangements. The father is represented by a flame-haired barrister in her mid-thirties, who takes herself very seriously, and is very correct and proper. The bench of three Magistrates; two women and one man, are sitting underneath the coat of arms of the United Kingdom; the lion and the unicorn, with the Latin motto "Honi soit qui mal y pense" – "Evil to him who thinks evil" - and are ready to hear the evidence from the father. The Clerk to the Court is sitting to their left to ensure the rules of procedure are correctly followed. The scene is set. I rise to my feet and ask the father, "On 16 June, the mother says you assaulted her by slapping her around the face. What do you say to that?" The father, a man in his late twenties or early thirties with gingerish dreadlocks, replies, "F★★★ off, w★★★er." I continue to put a series of questions to the father and his replies are interspersed with the above expletives and with the occasional, "T★★★er" thrown in. I am not disturbed by these words, nor are the Magistrates or the Clerk to the Court. Quite an extraordinary case. I had never come across Gilles de la Tourette's Syndrome previously. The father had filed with the Court medical evidence explaining his problem and the effect of it and his barrister had opened the case by explaining that there would be a number of expletives, usually repeated, but that it was not meant as insults or in the context that it was normally delivered and it was just a manifestation of the father's unfortunate condition. Once this was understood, the case went fine. Although it was nothing to do with his Tourette's syndrome, the Magistrates did find all twenty four allegations against the father proved, but he did get to see his child.

★

To be a successful high street lawyer dealing with mainly private clients on their family and financial matters, you have to like people generally and be interested in their problems and, yes, a bit nosey and inquisitive. Clients come in a whole range of ages, sizes, nationalities and attitudes and a lawyer has to adapt and deal with each person and each problem to suit their particular circumstances. There is no right or wrong way to do the job but initially there is the basic fact finding of name, address, occupation, date of birth etc and then, "Give me the headlines of the problem." More or less the first question we have to ask the client or potential client is their name. This seems straightforward but can produce some totally unanticipated results. A good friend of mine, John, was selling his bakery building and restaurant in the small market town of Bourne in Lincolnshire to his neighbour, a Chinese gentleman who ran a take-away business from the premises next-door to John. He wanted to purchase the bakery buildings to expand his own business. John told me he had given the Chinese gentleman, whose name was George, my telephone details and he was going to call me to give me the details I needed in relation to moving the transaction forward. Sure enough, a couple of days later a call was put through to me from George, who explained who he was. Although George had a strong Chinese accent, he was easy to understand and I told him I needed a few basic details to enable me to prepare the documentation relating to the sale of the bakery. "George," I said, "The first thing I need is your full name." He replied and I thought he said, "F★★k Y★u." I said, "Sorry, what did you say? Can you spell that?" George laughed and said, "That is why people call me 'George.' My name is Fuk Yau, spelt F-U-K Y-A-U, pronounced F★★k Y★u." We had a laugh together and he gave me the rest of his details. The story is true. A couple of weeks later, I had a call from a Mr Singh, who wanted us to deal with his off licence application for his shop. Again, I asked the standard question. "I know your last name is Singh. What is your first name?" "Buggar," he replied. We were also pursuing a personal injury claim for a young lad with the surname of Bates. The file was under the name of Master R. Bates. I called my secretary into my room and said to her, "Can you open a new file for Buggar Singh and put it next to the Fuk Yau file in the cabinet and bring me the Master Bates file." She did laugh. Sometimes, people who are film or music buffs do create some interesting names. A very good client is called John Wayne Lee, his brother's name is Elvis and his sister's name is Cher.

★

Another area which causes confusion and doubt in clients is asking them for their partner's or children's dates of birth. I remember being in an interview room with a client and I asked him the dates of birth of his children. He paused for a moment and said, "Wait a moment," and started taking his shirt off. I did not have a clue what he was up to but he then explained he had got his children's dates of birth and full names tattooed on his arm. Luckily, he only had two children otherwise he would have been struggling for body space! When I first started out in law at Nottinghamshire County Council, two of the senior solicitors were named Allan Merry and Richard Partridge. There was always a good party at Christmas at the general offices in West Bridgford. One particular year the signs on the office doors read "A Merry" with "Christmas" added after it and the office of R. Partridge had the 'R' changed to an 'A' and the words "in a pear tree" added. Excellent names for Christmas.

A very common family name in Cambridgeshire is Anker and I believe there is a local solicitor with that surname. Not too much imagination is needed to see what possibilities there are for the initials to go with the Anker surname. There is a well established and reputable firm of solicitors in Warwickshire known by a very distinctive name for lawyers involved in litigation – Wright Hassall LLP. According to their website, when Mr Wright and Mr Hassall renamed their firm in 1875, they could not have anticipated the linguistic evolution, which ensured the name of their firm would be etched in posterity! Another well established and reputable firm in Nottingham has a much cuddlier, fluffy name, as it was founded in 1992 by a solicitor called Rupert Bear. The firm is now known as Rupert Bear Murray Davies. My father-in-law was a haulage contractor and one of his drivers contacted me about the sale of his property. His name was Joseph Horace King. The sale price for the property was very low and he was selling to a friend and I asked him if he was serious about the transaction. He replied, "With a name like mine, do you think I would be Joe King?" The sale went through and Joe got his money.

A recent unusual surname we came across in the office was a young lady with the surname of 'World.' Imagine how lucky we were to have Miss World coming into the office. With a name like that I am sure she is not in a rush to get married.

★

It is often said that the UK and the USA are countries divided by a common language. For those of us in regular contact with our American cousins, there are plenty of examples of problems caused by our different uses of English. I think Americans probably have far more varied and unusual first names than the Brits and what seem unusual names to us do not cause them a problem. 'Randy' is an example which readily comes to mind. My wife's best friend from school, Suzanne, married an American called Don and they lived in Peterborough for many years. He ran a personnel consultancy business and did a lot of business in Italy. They decided to relocate to England to make Don's travelling to Italy a little easier and they rented some surplus office space from us. An employment recruitment consultancy also rented some surplus space from us and the three ladies employed in that business, Loretta, Val and Julie were all very friendly as was our American friend Don. One morning Suzanne was in the office and Val from the recruitment consultancy walked by their office on the way to her office. Don, being his normal friendly self, with a big smile on his face, shouted, "Hi Foul, how you doing?" Suzanne heard what Don had said and asked, "What did you just call that lady?" Don quite nonchalantly said "Foul, that is her name." Suzanne looked amazed, "No Don, her name is Val not Foul, and you must have misheard her." Don looked totally confused but I am sure he took on what Suzanne said as he commented, "I kinda thought Foul was an unusual name but if she calls herself Foul that must be her name!" The beauty of a common language.

★

Being in and around courts and clients and other lawyers is generally a very serious business but on rare occasions there are lighter moments. One such lighter moment occurred when I was due to appear on behalf of a client in Bedford Magistrates Court. The court building is in the middle of Bedford and is probably Victorian with numerous updates over the years. There are various court rooms and consultation rooms and a lawyers' room for the exclusive use of barristers and solicitors to hang their coats, leave their brief cases and use the usual facilities giving a little peace and quiet away from the clients. My case concerned an allegation of my client speeding and a possible disqualification as a consequence. The retention of her driving licence was important to her as she needed it for her work. I arrived at court in good time and saw the clerk to the court. She told me the case would be dealt with in ten minutes. I told the client and decided I needed a little comfort break before the case started. I nipped into the empty lawyers' room and then into the gents toilet at the far end of the room and shut and locked the door. I noticed the lock to the door was a bit loose and thought no more of it until I went to unlock the door - the lock would not turn! I was stuck. I looked around. There was no window so I could not attract any passers by outside so I started banging on the door and shouting. I knew there were no other people in the lawyers' room when I went in and it was likely there was nobody there now. In any event, nobody came to my aid. I stood there for a moment and thought – how embarrassing. I am due in court now to represent a client and here I am stuck in a toilet and nobody knows I am here. I banged and shouted again but no response. I then had a brainwave. I had my mobile telephone and there was a signal. I rang directory enquiries and asked to be put through to the office of the Clerk to the Justices. I was put through and a young lady answered the telephone and asked if she could help. I explained to her at the outset that this was a very unusual request and explained that I was locked in the toilet in the lawyers' room at Bedford Magistrates court. The lady was very sympathetic and said, "Don't go anywhere; I will get the court maintenance man." Anyway, about five minutes later, which seemed a long time to me, I heard a noise outside and then suddenly the door opened and a middle aged man with a screw driver and tool box was standing there. I thanked him profusely and he said, "No problem," and that the lock probably needed renewing as I was not the first person who had to be released in those circumstances. I thanked him and rushed by him straight into the court, got my client settled down and regained my composure and presented the case. Luckily my client was not disqualified and I am glad to say that this has been the only occasion where I have been locked up at court!

★

Some judges have formidable reputations and are very strict and stern and very correct and proper with formalities and procedures. Unfortunately, I found myself due to appear before such a judge at the Peterborough County Court in relation to a contact dispute between a mother and father in relation to their two young children. I was acting for the childrens' mother and a pleasant, young, female barrister named Miss Grewcock was acting for the childrens' father. Before going before the judge, Miss Grewcock and I had discussions as to whether there was any common ground or any way of resolving the differences between the parties without an acrimonious Court hearing with the parties giving evidence and being cross examined and the judge making the final decision. Both parent's positions were entrenched and therefore, there was no option but to go into Court and deal with the evidence before the judge. The parents, Miss Grewcock and I went into Court and the case started with Miss Grewcock opening and setting out her client's case. As she was speaking, it was clear to me and the judge that she was in some discomfort and when the judge enquired as to her wellbeing, she informed him that she was suffering from an appendicitis type stabbing pain in her stomach and she reluctantly conceded that she did not think she would be able to continue with the case. The judge was understandably very concerned as to her wellbeing and insisted that he himself would immediately take Miss Grewcock in his car to the nearby NHS Walk-in Centre. There was no further discussion and the case was adjourned. This was the first time I had ever been involved in a case that could not go ahead, not due to the illness of the judge or one of the parties, but due to the health of the opposing barrister. Nothing could be done and my client and her ex-partner just had to accept that the case of the upmost importance to them could not be dealt with now but they would have to reconvene in a couple of weeks. The judge and Miss Grewcock disappeared off to the NHS Walk in Centre. About half an hour later I was still in the Court waiting area trying to agree some revised contact arrangements between the parents pending the case coming back to Court. Suddenly and very unusually, the judge who had gone off with Miss Grewcock appeared in the waiting area looking a little flushed and agitated. He asked me if we could have a private word and I, of course, agreed. He asked me if I knew where the nearest NHS Walk-in Centre was and I said I did because I drove by it every day on my way to and from work. The judge replied that he knew where it was now on Thorpe Road, but he had gone into the clinic accompanied by Miss Grewcock which he believed was the Walk in Centre at Rivergate, only to be told that it was now the clinic for contraception and sexual health. I could just imagine the stern, red-faced judge accompanied by the young, attractive barrister walking out of the contraception and sexual health clinic. I did smile and I must admit I have recounted the story to a few colleagues who have encountered the wrath of the judge concerned.

★

As everybody knows and quite rightly expects, court proceedings are always conducted in a court room in a court building. However, unbelievably I recently took part in a court hearing before a District Judge with a barrister representing the other party where the venue was not a court room, but on the East Street pavement outside

Cambridge County Court with traffic driving past and pedestrians going about their everyday business. How did this extraordinary situation arise? That morning, a disgruntled defendant had attended the court in connection with his financial affairs and this person knew in advance that the case was not going to be decided in his favour. He therefore managed to sneak some flammable liquid in an ordinary plastic bottle of water past security guards at the entrance to the court. When his case was called into court, he walked in and sat down and then proceeded to empty the contents of the water bottle across the furniture between himself and the District Judge and set fire to it. The District Judge set off the fire alarm, all the court buildings were evacuated and the police and the fire brigade were called to deal with the situation. At this point, I was in a consultation room with my client and we heard the alarms. I assumed quite wrongly that it was a false alarm and we would soon be back so as my client and I vacated the building, I left my briefcase behind. After about three hours of standing outside in the street with all of the other court attendees, solicitors, barristers and judges, I was becoming very bored. Although the fire services were doing their best to get the situation under control, it appeared to me that we would not be back in the court building that day. I was talking to my opponent barrister about the case. In any event we both needed further information before we could proceed and the sensible way of dealing with the case was to have a fourteen day adjournment and come back to court with both parties equipped with the information needed. We located the District Judge dealing with our case milling around like the rest of us and asked him if he was prepared to deal with the matter. He said he had nothing else to be doing and therefore, despite the fact that we were in the street the Judge heard our application and granted the Order. The first and probably the only time I will be involved with "street justice!"

★

Marketing and advertising are subjects which solicitors find difficult to deal with and until fairly recently, solicitors were specifically prohibited from advertising. Consequently, even now solicitors' adverts in local lifestyle magazines are very dull and uninspiring and just tell you how friendly and efficient they are, and give a list of the subjects they deal with without any idea of the quality of the work and the price or any other information to inspire a potential client. A few years ago, we decided that we would be one of the first local firms of solicitors to advertise on local radio. The radio sales people and script writers came to see us and we discussed some ideas. At the time, the big story was the settlement of the financial dispute between Prince Charles and Princess Diana arising from the breakdown of their marriage. I suggested that we could open with some quotes from the wedding in 1981, then the announcement to parliament and the then Prime Minister, John Major, that they were to separate and then something along the lines of, "if you need advice on financial matters when your marriage breaks down, contact Terrells." Perhaps because I thought of it, I believed it was a good idea but the radio people thought it was a bad idea and potentially dangerous, as members of the public could be offended. We therefore ran with another idea, which I believe came from the radio scriptwriters. The US President, Bill Clinton, had been "exposed" in more ways than one for his relationship with the intern Monica Lewinsky. Hillary was not happy. The radio scriptwriters therefore suggested that the advertisement begin with traditional Sousa marching music and an announcement describing the President leaving his private jet, Airforce One, followed by the First Lady, the Second Lady and a Third lady whom he claims he has never met. The voiceover would then come in and say, "When your marriage goes wrong, contact Terrells Solicitors, telephone…" I thought that this was a great idea and we launched and ran with the advertisement for at least twelve months. However, perhaps due to my naivety in relation to potentially sensitive situations involving important or famous people, I did not realise or even think that anybody would be offended. I had obviously not taken account of Mrs Martin of Bretton, a suburb of Peterborough. She telephoned me most indignantly and informed me that she had heard our advertisement on the radio and she felt it was demeaning to the office of President of the United States of America by implying he was a serial philanderer. I was taken aback by the call, and unusually for me, I thought for a moment before I informed Mrs Martin that in my opinion, Bill Clinton had worked extremely hard on his own behalf to demean the office of President and we had not added or taken away from his reputation. Mrs Martin put the phone down without further comment and we heard nothing further from her.

★

Occasionally, we all see or hear advertisements which are really eye catching or clever. One of the best advertisements for legal services which I have ever seen was underneath the large score board clock at Valley Parade, the home of Bradford City Football Club. The clock is a prime location for any advertisement as supporters are always checking the clock to see how long their team has got left to score a goal or how long to last out without conceding another goal. Next to the clock were the words "Kama Sutra." I would guarantee that ninety-nine percent of spectators inside a football stadium would read further if they saw these words. This is exactly what I did… "Kama Sutra! When you find yourself in difficult positions contact us, Aurangzeb Iqbal Solicitors. Tel Bradford…" What a clever piece of advertising and name awareness. I have never been brave enough to incorporate this slogan into my advertising but subject to copyright, perhaps you could try it and see what response you get!

12. Everything Is Arranged

Asma Bibi was born in Mirpur, Azad Kashmir, Pakistan on 29 September 1985 and was a few minutes older than her twin sister. When she was very young, her father, mother, twin sister, and two older brothers moved to Karachi. Karachi is the former capital of Pakistan and now has a population estimated at fifteen million people. It is the country's largest city, largest seaport and its financial centre. It is a bustling, vibrant city. Asma was a carefree schoolgirl and grew up in this city with her family. She did well at school. One a day in April 2002, she came home from school. She was seventeen years old at the time. It was the end of the school term and school holiday time. Her father told her that they were going on a short holiday to visit his mother; her grandmother, back in Mirpur where the family originally came from. Although it was a long journey, Asma was looking forward to seeing her grandmother and to visit the place where her family came from. A few days later, Asma, her twin sister, and her father set off for Mirpur. Asma's mother could not travel with them as she had other commitments. After the long journey, the family arrived at Asma's grandmother's house in Azad Kashmir. Unbeknown to Asma, also staying at the grandmother's house were her aunty Parveen and her husband and their two adult sons. Parveen was the sister of Asma's father. Parveen and her family lived in Reading, England. Asma was told they were in Pakistan on holiday. Asma had never seen these people before and they were strangers to her. Asma only had a very limited grasp of the English language and she did not really have much to do with her uncle, aunty and cousins from England.

A couple of days later, Asma's father asked if he could have a private word with her. He told her that he had arranged with Parveen and her husband that Asma would marry their son, Mohammed. He was, of course, Asma's cousin, his mother was her aunty, her father was his uncle and they had the same grandmother. Asma was really upset. In fact, she was devastated. She had never spoken to her husband-to-be, Mohammed, and did not know anything about him, where he lived or what he did. She pleaded with her father to cancel the agreement but he was adamant that the marriage had to go ahead. Asma was only seventeen years old and if she refused to go ahead with the marriage, she would have no income, nowhere to live, and would be totally excluded from all contact with her family members. She also had an honest and genuine fear that her father would use violence against her, either to force her into the marriage or punish her for not going ahead with the marriage. Asma could not discuss the situation with her mother as she was back in Karachi. Asma did not say yes or no to the marriage but her view was irrelevant and the plans for the marriage went ahead regardless. Two days later, at 2.00pm, the marriage took place at The Jabeer Hotel in Mirpur, a very popular wedding venue. Asma had not spoken to her husband prior to the marriage. After the ceremony, there was a brief reception but Mohammed, his brother, and parents had to leave to get to the airport for their flight back to England. Asma, her father and sister returned to their home in Karachi.

Mohammed was an accountant and on his return to Reading he began the process of applying for a visa on behalf of his wife for her to join him in England. The first application he did himself but he did not include payslips and bank statements and it was rejected. Pending the granting of the visa, Mohammed and his family insisted that Asma return to her grandmother in Mirpur to live with her. Asma reluctantly agreed. The visa application was submitted a second time, this time via immigration lawyers. The family felt that Asma was perhaps too young and this might hinder her application. Therefore, her date of birth was changed from 1985 to 1983 on the application, making her two years older. For some reason, the second application was also rejected. A third application was made via another firm of specialist immigration lawyers and this application was finally successful.

Mohammed arranged for the tickets for Asma to fly to London, accompanied by an uncle. The visa process had taken seven months and Asma arrived in Reading at the end of January 2003 and went to Mohammed's family home in Reading, where the family lived together; mother, father, Mohammed, his brother and two sisters. Asma's aunty/mother-in-law controlled the household and Asma's passport, birth certificate, jewellery given to her as wedding presents and all her personal papers were taken from her. She was totally dependent on Mohammed and his family for food, housing and support. She soon realised that she was to be a virtual prisoner, not allowed out unless accompanied by a member of her husband's family and treated like a slave and expected to cook, clean, and wash for all members of the family. Her husband told her that he only married her to keep his parents happy. She soon fell pregnant and gave birth to three children in less than three and a half years. One significant issue of which she was never told was that her husband Mohammed was a schizophrenic. He was violent and suffered from delusions, which meant he could not work for long periods of time. When she told her in-laws of Mohammed's behavioural problems, they told her that she was his wife and it was now her duty to look after him. Asma was regularly subjected to violence from her husband in the presence of her young children. She was also assaulted by her aunty and female cousins and called "an uneducated paki" and a 'mangy', a derogatory term for the people coming to the UK from Pakistan.

Asma became desperate. Her family were still in Pakistan, although she did have some relatives living in Peterborough. Mohammed's family retained all her personal papers, including the children's birth certificates. She had no money and no support network and nobody she could turn to. Mohammed was, by this time, telling Asma that he was fed up with her and she should get out of his family's home and go back to Pakistan as she was an illegal immigrant as he had not done what he needed to do to ensure she had indefinite leave to remain. He told her the children would remain with him and his family, as the law in England favoured him because she was uneducated. Eventually, via her midwife, Asma made contact with a women's refuge and she made her escape with the children. She stayed in the refuge for a few weeks and then moved to be nearer her family members in Peterborough. Mohammed was incensed and called the police and social services. He alleged that Asma was not looking after the children properly. These allegations are of course very easy to make and the triggered responses from the authorities caused total anguish for Asma. However, both the police and social services visited and found that the children were of course totally well cared for and the allegations were false and made out of malice.

Asma consulted me. After finally getting her to reveal the true extent of her ordeal and gaining her trust, we obtained a Non-Molestation Order against her husband which prohibited him from using or threatening violence against her and pestering her. We also obtained a Residence Order for her three children to remain living with her, subject to them having regular staying contact with their father. We also obtained a financial settlement which has meant that Asma achieved secure housing and financial security for her children. Because of her young children, she could not work and is dependent on state benefits but she certainly hoped, in the future, to train in a career in nursing or teaching.

The large Pakistani population in Peterborough originates mainly from Azad Kashmir and the nearby Punjab area. The families are very close-knit and many still follow their tradition of arranged marriages to their first cousins and therefore, Asma's experience is very common. Either the wife has been born and brought up in England and goes to Pakistan to marry a first cousin or sometimes a more distant relative or the husband does the same. Of course, some marriages arranged in this way last forever and are very happy and successful. However, we see coming through our office unhappy spouses who are in a marriage they do not want, due to family pressure, implied or sometimes more explicit and threatening. The spouse coming from Pakistan often has a very limited ability to speak the English language and therefore struggles to obtain better employment and progress outside the Pakistani community. Once the relationship breaks down, there are often allegations of domestic violence, breaches of immigration rules and one party threatening to leave or take any children to Pakistan permanently. We also regularly hear stories from wives and their families who tell us that they married their cousin who had been born and educated in Peterborough. They arrived here to live with their husband's family and then they discovered he was into drugs and/or alcohol and had some mental health issue. Unfortunately, many spouses from Pakistan coming to England fail to check out their future spouse and make any real enquiries about their lifestyle and work etc. It is a tragedy for all the parties but it does happen regularly. In one very unusual and extreme case, a family's son was confined to a wheelchair with physical and mental difficulties but his family were still trying to find him a bride from Pakistan.

Lord Ahmed of Rotherham, Britain's first Muslim peer, has recently entered the debate in relation to first cousin marriages in the British Pakistani Community. Recent studies have shown that fifty-five percent of British Pakistanis marry their first cousins, usually from abroad. In Bradford, the figure is as high as seventy-five percent. Although marriage between first cousins is legal in Britain, it is frowned on by many and seen as a form of incest. The practice is illegal in thirty states of the USA. Lord Ahmed went further and linked arranged marriages to young Pakistani men preying on vulnerable, young white girls to fulfil their sexual needs. Lord Ahmed wants an end to marriages between cousins and says, "They are forced into marriages and they are not happy. They are married to girls from overseas who they do not have anything in common with, and they have children and a family, but they are looking for fun in their sexual activities and seek out vulnerable girls." He said Asian men resort to abusing young white girls because they do not want meaningful relationships with adult white women. "An adult woman – if you are having an affair – would want your time, money and for you to break up your marriage", the peer added. His comments came weeks after former Foreign Secretary Jack Straw provoked national outrage by saying that some Pakistani men look at white girls as 'easy meat' for sexual abuse. Labour peer Lord Ahmed said, "I get a lot of criticism from Asian people who ask, "How can you say this about Asian men?" But they must wake up and realise there is a problem. I am deeply worried about this as it has happened in my own backyard, and in Rochdale and Bradford. This did not happen in my father's generation. This is happening among young Asians. While I respect individual choice, I think the community needs to look at marriages in the UK rather than cousin marriages or economic marriages from abroad."

Academics and journalists have now become involved in the debate regarding genetic problems caused by first cousin marriages. In May 2011, The Daily Telegraph carried a news headline of, "Professor risks political storm over Muslim inbreeding." The article then set out how Professor Steven Jones of University College, London was likely to find himself in the centre of controversy as a result of his comments regarding the level of inbreeding among Muslims in Britain and how this was endangering the health of future generations. Research in Bradford had found that babies born to Pakistani women are twice as likely to die in the first year as babies born to white mothers, with genetic problems linked to inbreeding identified as a significant cause. Separate studies have found that white British Pakistanis make up three percent of all births they account for, one in three children born with genetic illnesses. The article then went on to explore genetic problems caused by inbreeding in royal families and families in fairly isolated communities such as Northern Ireland and the Outer Hebrides. The debate was then fuelled by an article by Saira Khan, the former 'The Apprentice' contestant and Muslim TV Presenter. She described how she had witnessed at first hand genetic disabilities in the Muslim community, from blindness and hearing problems to blood disorders, but in this politically correct age, the subject is taboo with precious few people willing to speak out for fear of being branded Islamaphobic and causing offence, rather than concern for the plight of the poor, blameless children. She described how many Muslims born in Britain are under intense family pressure to "marry within" as a way of keeping money within the family. If they do not, they face being ostracised by their own relatives. Apparently, the practice has been common for hundreds of years. Whilst it may be happening among poor, uneducated villagers halfway round the world; there is no excuse for it in a modern advanced country like Britain. Several national newspapers have picked up on the theme and tried to open up the debate.

Another problem we see regularly is when white middle aged British men meet their brides to be on the internet. The potential brides can be from any country, but are predominantly from the former Eastern bloc countries of Eastern Europe or Thailand, China and the Philippines. The men visit the brides in their own countries and often the brides do not speak or have a very limited knowledge of English but agree to marry and live in the UK with their husband. Very soon after the marriage a child comes along and then in the cases we see, the parties fall out, the wife denies the husband contact with the child and the husband challenges the wife's immigration status and tries to have her deported with the child remaining in the UK living with him.

In many cultures marriage is permitted at a younger age than in England. A person may marry in England at the age of sixteen with parental consent and obviously at eighteen without consent. I acted for a Bengali family whose fifteen year old daughter was taken into care by Northamptonshire County Council, as it was believed that the parents were going to take their daughter out of school and travel to Bangladesh for her to marry a relative in an arranged marriage. Eventually, we managed to persuade the Local Authority and the Court that the planned trip to Bangladesh was just to visit relatives and not to marry, but there are unfortunately too many cases of young girls being taken abroad by their families and forced into marriage against their will.

13. More of The Same?

W hen I first set up my high street solicitors practice back in 1988, the majority of solicitors were white, middle aged, middle class and male. The high streets in the towns and cities up and down Britain were populated by plenty of small, one to five partner firms. The solicitors in these firms would often be well known and well respected in their locality and be involved with municipal politics and charity work such as Rotary and Round Table. Many local families would have used the same firm of solicitors for generations and would never think of going elsewhere for their legal services. All solicitors firms were able to carry out publicly funded work (legal aid), if they so wished and criminal and civil work, including personal injury claims. Advertising and marketing had recently become possible but many firms were uncomfortable with marketing their services as this was considered not to be in keeping with the professional image of solicitors. Once qualified, there was no compulsory on-going training and clients were very respectful and reluctant to complain even when such a complaint may well have been justified. Many high street solicitors were not specialists in any particular area of law but were Jacks (or Jills) of all trades appearing in the Magistrates Court on a criminal matter in the morning and going back to the office in the afternoon and drafting a conveyance or a will. Most small towns had a local Magistrates Court and a County Court. There was technology with electronic typewriters, fax machines and photocopiers, but the pace of legal life was relatively sedate, civilised and friendly. None of us in particular like change; we like to do things in a way we are comfortable with and the way we have always done them. Fortunately or unfortunately, the subsequent years since 1988 have seen unprecedented change in the legal and all other professions. The challenge has been how to adapt and deal with these extensive and far reaching changes. Many of these changes have been positive and have substantially improved the profession and how legal services have been delivered to the public. Some changes inevitably have had the opposite effect.

Without a doubt, a positive change has been developments in technology, which has substantially improved the speed and quality of written and oral communication and reduced the cost to the client. Immediate examples which spring to mind are court hearings relating to conduct of cases before the courts being conducted over the telephone with three way conference calls, and evidence being given in cases by video links to judges and the courts. The opportunities for entry into the profession are greater and open to a wider audience with the growth of universities providing courses leading to a degree in pure law or a combined degree. I often cynically joke with my staff when we review the latest batch of CVs for training contracts that applicants have a degree in law and scuba diving or law and flower arranging. The growth in the number of law courses has resulted in a huge increase to the number of qualified solicitors, particularly females, and both males and females from ethnic groups. However, the downside of this situation is that there is now a huge pool of well educated, well motivated people who have no chance of ever becoming a solicitor or barrister because market forces dictate that there are just not enough opportunities. Recently, we recruited a receptionist who had a Law Degree and also a Masters Degree in family law. The lady in question was prepared to take a job at that level despite her qualifications just to get a foothold in and experience a high street solicitors practice. The procedures and processes of legal work have also substantially changed with organisations such as the Land Registry, Probate Registry and particularly courts and tribunals streamlining and improving their ways of doing business by the use of technology and the provision for documents to be submitted "online." Solicitors can no longer be "all-rounders." It is virtually impossible to keep up to date with changes in the law and procedures, in both criminal and family law for example. Therefore, even in small firms, solicitors are much more specialised and competent in their chosen area, aided by compulsory education at an absolute minimum of sixteen hours of training in every calendar year. The Law Society has also introduced quality standards whereby the public are able to have some idea whether the solicitor they intend to instruct has knowledge and experience in a particular area of law, such as the Family Law Panel or Personal Injury Panel. In addition, the Law Society has developed a professional quality standard for firms of solicitors known as Lexcel, again to give the public some information or indication as to the level of quality achieved in their prospective solicitors. Now, only firms of solicitors who have met fairly stringent qualifying conditions can provide publicly funded work to the clients. All other firms are excluded from providing this service, which was never the case previously.

The demographics of clients have changed considerably. In our Peterborough office family law department, we did a quick survey recently and one fee earner had taken on clients from fourteen different nationalities, many not speaking English at all or with very limited English language skills. This has resulted in a huge increase in the use of interpreters and the attendant costs. There has also been a huge increase in the white underclass with young women having one or more children at a young age with different fathers, and families who for two or three generations have not had the head of the household in paid employment. Marriage has declined and relationships are much more transient.

Clients who are subjected to domestic violence are a huge feature of many high street practices dealing with family and criminal law and the work of the civil and criminal courts. There have been a number of initiatives over the years and in my experience the police respond quickly and deal effectively with violence in domestic situations but it is still a huge problem fuelled often by alcohol or drugs. In dealing with clients with family problems relating to finances and children, it is easy to get a distorted view of the world and believe that domestic violence, contact with children and finance arguments affect everybody. They do not and we only see a very small but polarised section of the community with immediate, urgent and distressing problems. The majority of the community are quite happy in their relationships or resolve their issues and differences themselves. The ingenuity and creativity of ordinary people to create problems for themselves and those around and close to them does not and will not change and is not affected by race or gender or financial circumstances.

There has definitely become a marked deterioration in standards and respect for authority. Many people turn up to civil, family and criminal courts dressed in a baseball cap, t-shirt, jeans and trainers. These are perhaps the only type of clothes they possess but in the past, there was definitely a culture of trying to put on smart clothes when appearing before a court. Another negative aspect is the willingness at every stage for a person involved in the judicial system to complain about the solicitor, the barrister, the police or any other person they come into contact with. Some complaints are obviously proper and justified but many are made because the person does not like the particular outcome and its effect on them.

A negative aspect of changes over the years has been the development of political correctness in all areas of society, particularly the government, and the legal profession is not exempt. My practice is situated in Cambridgeshire. Our Legal Services Commission area office is in Cambridge and our staff need to telephone them regularly regarding applications we have made on behalf of our clients for public funding. As soon as we telephone, the first, or one of the first options we are given, is to conduct the telephone call in Welsh. We are not in Cardiff or Wrexham, so why would we want this option? How many callers exercise this option? I will have to make an enquiry under the Freedom of Information Act. For our clients to be granted public funding they have to quite rightly and understandably fill in voluminous forms detailing obvious information details such as name, address, ethnic group and gender etc. However, under the heading of 'gender' they have not two but three options. The obvious options of male and female are there, but also a third option of "prefer not to say." Now, we complete hundreds of applications for public funding on behalf of both males and females, all of who have been quite happy to state their gender. Sometime in the future we may have a client who would prefer not to say, but to date, this has not happened.

The legal profession has been opened up to fierce competition amongst solicitors firms and now other organisations under the recent Legal Services Act. In the past, solicitors would act for their own clients in connection with personal injury matters arising from road traffic accidents, accidents at work or slipping and tripping on pavements. Now there is a whole industry of claims handlers and referrers who initially recruit the client via high street shop fronts, television, newspapers, Yellow Pages advertisements, advertisements in NHS casualty departments, GP surgeries and various other sources. They then "sell" the claim to the highest bidding firm of solicitors who conduct the case on a "No Win No Fee" basis and recover their lucrative fees plus a success fee from the insurers of the person responsible for the accident. Consequently, we find that our existing clients are being represented by firms of solicitors they never see in places such as Liverpool or Manchester. Referral fees are now very commonly charged by estate agents referring conveyancing work to solicitors. Many such estate agents do not make it clear to their customers that they will be paid a referral fee and they imply that if the client is to get the house they want and the transaction is to go through smoothly and quickly, the client must use the solicitor the estate agent nominates. Again, the traditional high street firm is losing out and it seems that the only organisation benefiting is the estate agent.

There is a continued threat of what is commonly referred to as "Tesco Law," where well known brand names with huge customer loyalty and very strong brands such as Tesco's, big insurance companies and big banks are providing legal advice, particularly in areas of work such as wills, probate, conveyancing and personal injury claims. These well respected, well financed organisations could do real damage to the traditional high street solicitors if they came into the market with well organised specialist services with a heavy dependence on technology. However, a well-run, well-organised high street practice is difficult to compete against as they are much more nimble and still do have client loyalty and an ability to deal with the distressing problems generated by relationship breakdowns or allegations of criminal behaviour.

On a recent family holiday to North America, I was walking past a specialist shop just selling t-shirts with slogans emblazoned across the front. One t-shirt in particular caught my eye, - the slogan was "A Good Lawyer Knows The Law – A Successful Lawyer Knows the Judge." This slogan made me pause for a while and think about my own experience, having spent a large part of my career regularly appearing before Circuit Judges and District Judges, Chairmen/Chairwomen of Employment Tribunals and Magistrates. For the sake of ease, I shall call them all judges. I could not miss this opportunity to set out my views. Most judges are experienced barristers or solicitors who have spent most of their careers before becoming a judge appearing on behalf of clients in the court room. They are therefore experienced advocates and have experienced at first hand the majority of scenarios likely to occur before a court and they will have a good working knowledge of the law. As it takes several years to reach the stage of having the necessary qualifications to be a judge, most judges are still white, middle class and predominantly male. One consistent feature of a judge is their inconsistency. Go before one judge in one court with a set of facts and receive a decision, go before another judge in another court with exactly the same facts and receive a completely different decision. This inconsistency creates a real problem in advising clients as to the likely outcome of their cases unless of course you know the judge and then you have a real chance of advising the client with certainty as to the likely outcome of their case. Judges are always worried about the implications of the Human Rights Act and giving litigants before them a proper hearing and opportunity to say their piece. This problem is really exacerbated by the growing trend in civil and family cases for litigants to be in person, who starts off by asserting their ignorance of the law and court procedures. Consequently, such persons can say or do more or less as they please, whereas solicitors and barristers are governed by rules of etiquette and procedure and are much more constrained. In the selection of judges there does not seem to be any personality or client care test. Consequently, judges exhibit the whole range of attributes we see and experience in life as general, from judges who are extremely polite and courteous to judges who are rude and ignorant. I personally believe a judge should be selected for the former attributes and not the latter. I have known a young female barrister appearing before a judge and becoming so distressed by his rude manner that she has burst into tears and rushed out to the toilet to collect herself together and in the meantime the judge has had to adjourn the case. Perhaps the barrister in question should have had more fortitude but such rudeness is totally inappropriate but does occur quite often. Judges do have an unenviable task in civil and family matters as often one or both of the parties appearing before the court are totally unreasonable and unrealistic in their expectations and that is why the matter cannot be resolved without a court hearing. Unfortunately, it falls to the judge to make a decision, but I do feel there are better ways of preparing litigants for likely outcomes, particularly in matters concerning their children.

I have had a wonderful opportunity to practice as a lawyer in various fields of work, from a large local authority, a legal advisor in industry and through to a high street solicitor dealing with peoples' everyday problems and crises and, on occasions, much more serious matters. Have I enjoyed it? Yes, of course I have. Am I optimistic for the future? Yes, of course I am. Despite continued change and threats, it is in everybody's interest to have a strong, independent, accessible legal profession. I look forward to more of the same!

Index